SLAPSHOT!

By the Same Author

GORDIE HOWE
BOBBY ORR AND THE BIG, BAD BRUINS
STRANGE BUT TRUE HOCKEY STORIES
STAN MIKITA: THE TURBULENT CAREER OF A
HOCKEY SUPERSTAR
I'VE GOT TO BE ME
(Derek Sanderson and Stan Fischler)
PLAY THE MAN
(Brad Park and Stan Fischler)
THE FLYING FRENCHMEN:
HOCKEY'S GREATEST DYNASTY
(Maurice Richard and Stan Fischler)

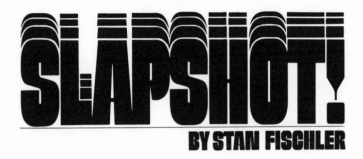

SLAPSHOT!

BY STAN FISCHLER

GROSSET & DUNLAP
A National General Company
PUBLISHERS   NEW YORK

Dedication

Contrary to what many of my readers and critics may believe, I still love the game of hockey and a number of the players and others connected with it. This book is dedicated to those who have made my years with the sport more enjoyable either by their behavior on the ice, in the dressing room, or across an interview table:

Carl Brewer, Frank Mahovlich, Maurice Richard, Frank Boucher, Aldo Guidolin, Larry Zeidel, Bobby Hull, Wally Hergesheimer, Nick Mickoski, Marv Albert, Nick Pidsodny, Muzz Murray, Art Coulter, Foster Hewitt, Al Albert, Doug Smith, Danny Gallivan, Baz O'Meara, Elmer Ferguson, Gordie Howe, Henri Richard, Don Raleigh, Max Bentley, Bill Ezinicki, Syl Apps, Sr., Dennis Murphy, Neil Shayne, Ron Ward, Bob Woolf, Ken Hodge, Jim Coleman, Vern DeGeer, Camille Henry, Fishy Dumond, Ty Anderson, Dalton MacArthur, Arthur Reichert, Gladys Goodding, Tom Lockhart, Ebbie Goodfellow, Bobby Hewitson, Johnny Wilson, Ira Gitler, Leo Coar, Paul Gardella, Sy Adelson, Stan Saplin, Herb Goren, Paul Ronty, Eddie Kullman, Jack Gordon, Joe Breu, Frank Traverso, Bert Lee, Sr., Bert Lee, Jr., Ward Wilson, Mickey Slowik, King Clancy, Howie Meeker, Floyd Curry, Paul Waldner, Manny Cotlow, Doug Bentley, Joe Nichols, Jim Burchard, Marvin Milkes, Trent Frayne, Ralph Allen, Milt Dunnell, Jim Proudfoot, Dan Proudfoot, Al Nickelson, Court Benson, Wes McKnight, Hal Cotton, Wren Blair, John Ferguson, Ed Van Impe, Les Binkley, Gump Worsley, Cesare Maniago, Bob Verdi, Tim Burke, John Robertson, Claude Larochelle, Charlie Barton, Lou Fontinato, Carl Glickman, Jack Goldstein, Dave Perlmutter, Edgar Laprade, Jim Hernon, Bert Korwin, Arnie Fox, Doug Harvey, Reg Sinclair, Bob Stampleman, T.J. Rugg, Max McNab, Andy Hebenton, Andy Bathgate, Reg Fleming, Glenn Hall, Sam B. Gunst.

TABLE OF CONTENTS

SLAPSHOT!

I

THE MAKING
OF A
TROUBLEMAKER

I was probably destined to be a film critic. But my father wouldn't cooperate.

It was November 1938. My dad and I were en route to the Globe Theater in Times Square and the first-run showing of Walt Disney's *Snow White and the Seven Dwarfs*.

There have been few events in my lifetime which I've anticipated with more enthusiasm than I did that movie. (My Bar Mitzvah was another, only because my Hebrew teacher primed me to such a pitch that I felt supremely "up" for my big performance. I didn't win an Oscar but I did come away with two fountain pens which, in those days, were worth *four* Oscars. Especially since one was an Esterbrook!)

To reach the Globe Theater from our house in the Williamsburgh section of Brooklyn, we took the subway to the Eighth Avenue and 50th Street station, next to the old Madison Square Garden. This put us five blocks away from the Globe or, as my father said when we got there, "Five blocks too many."

The problem was simple enough; he hadn't brought an umbrella and a torrential downpour had suddenly hit Manhattan. As we stood at the dripping station exit, my father looked up at the marquee overhead and uttered the words that would chart the route of my life for the next 35 years.

"Y'know," Dad said in a tone that omened disaster for me, "we're not going to see *Snow White and the Seven Dwarfs*. I'm taking you to see a hockey game!"

From what I knew of hockey, he might have said he was taking me to see the Dalai Lama. All that mattered was that Snow White had been knocked out of the box and that meant catastrophe to a six-year-old; so I cried.

My father had a rather inflexible position toward bawling brats. He would do the opposite of what the kid was crying for. In this case it meant we went to the hockey game. With a tug of my arm, we walked under the Garden marquee which said: *"THIS AFTERNOON, EASTERN LEAGUE HOCKEY—NEW YORK ROVERS VS. WASHINGTON EAGLES."* In we went.

Sensing the inevitability of it all, and not appreciating it one bit, I decided at least to look around. Almost immediately, I was dazzled by the sight below our mezzanine seats. The milky-white ice was graced by ten skaters. One team wore bright red jerseys with a large "R" on the front; the other had spanking white uniforms and an especially fleet skater with splendid golden hair. For reasons best known to my psyche, I dubbed him The Lone Ranger and hoped he would do heroic things in the two hours ahead.

As luck would have it my Lone Ranger turned out to be Normie Burns of the Washington Eagles, a player of extraordinary talent who skittered around the rink like a water bug on a pond. He not only looked wonderful; everything he did was wonderful and that bothered my Dad a great deal, who was rooting for the home team, the Rovers.

I hadn't forgiven my father for switching from *Snow White* to the game and decided early on that if he was rooting for the Rovers I would cheer for the other team. The fact that Normie Burns was playing so well, and Washington was running away with the victory, made it all the more delicious. As we walked out of the Garden, two and a half hours after my sobbing scene, I told my Dad to forget *Snow White*. "I want to see another hockey game next Sunday."

The Eastern League, a minor league which was a feeder for the NHL, included teams with a lot of bird names—Eagles of Washington, Falcons of Philadelphia, Orioles of Baltimore—and briefly a team with the unlikely name of the River Vale Skeeters, as well as New York's Rovers and others. The Rovers had the Garden ice every Sunday afternoon, and although my father was not what you would call an avid hockey fan, he had followed the Rangers and the New York Americans (New York's other NHL team, which folded in 1942). The idea of taking me to another Sunday afternoon match was quite all right with him, since Rover tickets were much cheaper than Ranger tickets; and since my Dad was making less than $35 a week, every dollar saved was meaningful to us. Thus began what was to be a long series of wonderful Sunday afternoons at the Garden.

Having established my position as an anti-Rovers (anti-father) rooter during our first game I felt obliged to maintain my stance. On the following Sunday the Baltimore Orioles were in town. Unfortunately they didn't have a Normie Burns on their team but they did have magnificently colored uniforms; light brown on dark brown with a large bird crest on the front.

During the first game I rooted against my Dad. This time

5

I noted with some dismay that the 10,000 fans *all* seemed to be cheering for the Rovers and against the handsomely outfitted visitors. I regarded this as a one-sided and illogical point of view on esthetic and hospitable grounds. Why, I wondered, should all these people root for New York if all of the players came from Canada? The answer—that the Rovers wore New York uniforms—did not satisfy me and thereafter I rooted not only against my Dad but against the Garden spectators. It was a rather hefty undertaking for a lad of six but I felt up to it.

My father treated my hockey mania as a passing fancy which would disappear eventually at the end of the hockey season. However the arrival of April and the warm breath of spring plunged me into a long depression which was only lifted by the arrival of October and the new hockey season.

I didn't get into hockey reporting until the second grade when my teacher at Public School 54, a wonderful lady named Mrs. Gould, gave us an assignment called "Show and Tell."

By this time I had become totally obsessed with the hockey goaltender—I'm *sure* there's something Freudian in that—especially his big, fat leather leg pads and his job of stopping that hard rubber puck from entering the odd-shaped net.

On the Monday following a particularly exciting game between the Rovers and the Boston Olympics, I volunteered to do a "Show And Tell" on Maurice Courteau, the Olympics goalie who not only was very good but wore his hair like movie idol Robert Taylor. For the Tell part, I explained the difficulty of the goalie's job, and wound up with an attempt to do a perfect split in front of the class for the Show part. Mrs. Gould was good enough to help me off the floor and reward me with an A.

From that day on, I realized that there was a lot to be gained just by talking hockey. It never dawned on me that one could be paid for broadcasting or writing about the sport. For that privilege, one should do it for nothing.

Up to March 1942 my hockey horizons had been limited to Rover (Eastern League) games at the Garden and Metropolitan Amateur League contests which were played as preliminaries to the Rover games, and which I frequently enjoyed just as much as the speedier Rover matches.

I had heard about, and occasionally read about, the National Hockey League and knew enough to root against the Rangers simply because they were parents to the Rovers. But I had not yet come up with a favorite NHL team until the arrival of my tenth birthday and a gift from my parents.

It was a tiny Philco Transitone table radio, measuring about eight inches long and six inches high. The set was so small, in fact, one could hardly imagine it picking up all the New York stations, let alone any out-of-town broadcasts. But one Saturday night early in April I turned the toothpick-thin red dial and suddenly heard the staccato-like voice of a man broadcasting a hockey game.

There was a peculiar quality about this man's style. It generated a pleasant brand of tension as it flowed with the waves of attack and defense and it achieved the ultimate vocal climax when a goal was scored. This fellow, Foster Hewitt, would start the crescendo by half-yelling, HE SHOOTS! and then completing the aural orgasm with *HE SCORES!!* The peculiar thrill of hearing him complete the play sent me climbing the walls with joy.

But it was more than that. There was something about the Toronto Maple Leafs as a hockey team that appealed to me as much as Foster Hewitt's play-by-play. They had names that tickled my ear. Names like Wally Stanowski, Gordie Drillon, Syl Apps, Turk Broda, Bingo Kampman—who, I later learned, was so strong he could lift a heavy table by placing the end of it between his huge

7

teeth—Sweeney Schriner, Lorne Carr and Bucko Mc-Donald. It was impossible not to love this team.

Except that the Maple Leafs were in the Stanley Cup (I was rather pleased to learn the name of the championship trophy was the same as mine) finals and had fallen behind the Detroit Red Wings, three games to none. One more loss and the Maple Leafs would lose the cup.

What direction my rooting support would have taken had the Leafs lost, I cannot guess, nor does it really matter. Toronto proceeded to do what no other NHL team has done before or since. They won the next four straight games and, of course, the Stanley Cup! By the time the seventh game was over I had become a diehard Toronto Maple Leaf fan and would remain so until September 1954 when I was hired to work for the Rangers.

Unfortunately for me, the Maple Leaf-Ranger games at the Garden were held in the evening, starting at 8:30. My parents adamantly refused to allow me out at night—"you're too young" was their narrow-minded explanation—which meant that I would obtain my minimal weekly requirement of hockey by watching the Rovers and their foes.

After two years of escorting me to the Rover matches, my father decided that he'd had enough. I now needed a new partner and found one at school. He was Larry Schildkret, a chubby lad who happened to have an excellent singing voice. I know this for a fact because I heard and saw Larry sing "Apple Blossom Time" during the intermission of a Rover game when organist Gladys Goodding conducted amateur hours.

Larry not only liked singing, he liked hockey as well. However, neither his parents nor mine were quite willing to pay for weekly tickets, money still being tight in our respective houses. Luckily, my mother had become a member of the 79th Police Precinct Community Council just at the time the Police Athletic League had made a deal with the Rovers. Each week the PAL received several thousand free tickets to distribute among the PAL branches. Mother learned of this and managed to obtain a dozen or so tickets to every Rover game from the local precinct commander. Larry Schildkret and I were in!

Each Sunday morning we'd meet at the Myrtle-Willoughby subway station of the IND Brooklyn-Queens crosstown subway line and cram ourselves under the automatic turnstile, thereby saving ten cents right off the bat. Normally we'd be on the GG local train at 11 A. M., arriving at the Garden by 11:30 A. M. We considered it our duty to be among the first dozen kids in line so that we were assured of a front row balcony seat. We rarely missed.

This automatically created problems since we were doing our thing in mid-winter and the Garden never opened its doors until about 12:45. The January and February Sunday mornings were the worst. It was not unusual for the temperature to dip to 10 or 15 degrees, making life more than miserable along windy 49th Street.

To distract ourselves from the cold, Larry and I usually brought along pounds of newspapers, comic books and magazines; anything to read until the doors opened. When, at last, the glorious moment finally arrived—signaled by the sudden appearance of four gray-uniformed Garden policemen—we primed ourselves the way middle-distance runners do at the start of a race. For now, although we had first position, the real challenge came; the race from box-office level to the top of the Garden balcony and then the precarious dance down the cliff-like steps to the front row seats.

Being thinner, taller and considerably faster than Larry, I took the steps two and three at a time and frequently reached the top before any of the other scrambling maniacs. I never was quite as good going down as I was climbing the stairs so I usually wound up in the front row after two or three other lads had passed me by. No matter. I got there in time to preserve my seat and save one for Larry who arrived a half-minute later. Securing seats in that manner had all the gratification of finishing among the top three in an Olympic race. Only occasionally did Larry and I fail, thereby being relegated to the second or third rows.

For reasons that I never could determine, Larry also was an anti-Rover rooter; a fact which made us eminently compatible. We also shared the same favorites in the Met League that played the preliminary games. We remained hockey partners through the World War II years, from 1941 through 1945.

Missing a Rover game was out of the question. I regarded it with the same devotion and obligation as a sailor assigned to submarine-scouting from his position in the crow's nest of a destroyer. There was absolutely no question of not doing the job—not going to the game. As a result I was compelled to quit the Boy Scouts after learning that Troop 320 conducted its hikes on Sunday afternoons, when the hockey games were on. The Boy Scouts never had a chance.

Perhaps the most awesome calamity in those early hockey-watching days occurred early one season when I learned that my grandparents would celebrate their fiftieth anniversary with a gala family party on a Sunday afternoon in February.

Egad! This could be a matter of life or death. I dashed to my room, found the Rovers' home schedule and found that my fears were confirmed—there *was* a Rover home game on the afternoon of the anniversary party! I could not under any circumstances miss the hockey game—the Rovers were playing the Philadelphia Falcons, one of my favorite teams—and I certainly could not miss the anniversary party.

What to do?

One possibility I considered was hiring a stand-in who looked like me and have him represent me at the grandparents' party until the hockey game was over. Another was to urge my uncles and aunts who were planning the gala to have it at the Hotel Belvedere, across the street from the Garden. I could then attend the game and visit the party between periods.

Unfortunately, these and other brainstorms were rejected and after consultations with a few respected relatives I concluded there really was no way I could miss the party. How, then, would I be able to face Larry Schildkret? How could I explain this abject defection? More to the point, how would I be able to live if I missed the hockey game? Glumly, I went to the party.

The outcome left me with a mixture of pleasure and depression. I was delighted on the following morning to discover that I still was breathing. And, after picking up a copy of the New York *Herald-Tribune* I learned that the Rovers (ech!) had defeated the Falcons and I was rather upset; not so much by the result of the game but by the fact that I really didn't miss that much after all. For one brief day I realized that I *could* survive without hockey. However, the feeling didn't last very long.

The war years were an exciting time for me, approaching my teens. A community spirit swept over our neighborhood in Williamsburgh. The corner candy store window was sprinkled with photos of our local heroes in the Armed Forces and the strains of "Anchors Aweigh" and "The Marine's Hymn" were frequently whistled on the walks to and from school.

The war years also played a role in my hockey rooting thanks to a team called the Coast Guard Cutters, organized by the Coast Guard at its base near Baltimore. The team played in the Eastern League and its members were major and minor leaguers who were serving in the Coast Guard. They included such aces as goalie Frankie Brimsek of the Boston Bruins, Johnny Mariucci of the Chicago Black Hawks and Art Coulter of the Rangers. But they also had some lesser-known skaters who, somehow, had even more appeal for me.

I was absolutely entranced by the other Coast Guard goalie, Muzz Murray, by a Jewish defenseman named Manny Cotlow and by forwards Joe Kucler and Bob Gilray. For an anti-Rover fan, the Coast Guard Cutters were a dream because they were so much better than the ordinary Eastern League team, particularly the Rovers. On top of that, the Cutters sported absolutely magnificent uniforms. Their jerseys had a blue ground with a huge red and white cross-anchored emblem in front while white stars adorned the shoulders and arms. Because of their rough but dazzling style, they were alternately called "Hooligan's Navy" or "The Star Spangled Skaters." Either way, I loved them passionately and prayed, I'm afraid, that the war would never end.

What also made the Cutters' visits such a delight was their enormous 60-piece band. Nestled comfortably in the Garden's end arena, the Cutters' band lent a college-football gaiety to the proceedings. Whenever the Coast Guard scored a goal, the band would launch into "Semper Paratus," the Coast Guard marching song, which to me is the most stirring military march ever written. Hearing them play "Semper Paratus" following a goal was more gratifying than getting a new set of electric trains.

But, alas, the war did end and the Cutters disappeared. I never thought I'd be as infatuated with another team and, in a sense I was right, although the Cutters' successor in Baltimore, the Blades, turned out to be a surprisingly intriguing team for different reasons.

Unlike the Cutters, Baltimore's Blades wore the most uncomplicated uniforms I've ever seen. The jerseys were plain white with B-L-A-D-E-S sewn in remarkably small letters at a 45-degree angle across the front. But on them it looked good, perhaps because they were a good hockey team. Not as good as the Cutters, nor as colorful, but they carried two players who replaced Muzz Murray and Manny Cotlow on my personal hit parade. The goalie was Nick Pidsodny. The defenseman was Paul Waldner.

Pidsodny had a name and a nose that mesmerized me. It wasn't a particularly long nose but it had an arrowhead quality about it that I plain liked. And how can anyone not like a goalie named Pidsodny?

His defenseman, Paul Waldner, was nicknamed "Boxcar" for obvious reasons. He was built like a fireplug and took great delight in smashing the Rovers into the ice. The Blades had a few other good men—I remember a swift forward named Arly Carlson—and were competent enough to enable me to forget the Coast Guard Cutters in due time.

With each birthday, I drew closer and closer to the night when I would be old enough to attend a Rangers game at 8:30. My parents cleverly avoided setting a specific date, but one afternoon in 1944 I pressed my father about taking me to see the Rangers against the Chicago Black Hawks that night. To my surprise he agreed but, ironically, as dinnertime arrived, a heavy rain developed and he began to reconsider. I worked over him long and hard enough to clinch the deal and out into the downpour we went.

That first NHL game was a total letdown. Our seats were high in the side balcony where a quarter of the ice was obstructed from view. To my dismay the NHL players did not skate any faster than the Eastern Leaguers had, and as if that wasn't tragedy enough, the Rangers—who I was against of course—beat Chicago by a goal. Anyway, I'd made a breakthrough even though I wasn't sure the game was much to cheer about.

The war's end meant a strengthening of the Rovers since they were a Rangers farm team and many ex-Rangers were returning from the armed forces and getting into NHL shape by working out with the Eastern League club. Until then, I had been coping with the overwhelming odds of a pro-Rovers audience by using my lung power. But sometime in 1946 I discovered an old cowbell in our house and remembered that Hilda Chester, the famous Brooklyn Dodger rooter, had used a cowbell to root home her "Bums." That year the cowbell became an integral part of my rooting repertoire along with three tangerines which my mother graciously inserted in the food package she gave me for every game. (It also contained a sandwich, two black olives and three Toll House cookies).

The tangerines served a dual purpose. They were delicious eating, but they also made excellent missiles for tossing at errant referees. If they hit the official—I never was quite *that* accurate—they were too soft to hurt him, and if they missed they splattered beautifully on the ice. Orange on white always was a nifty combination.

One of the pleasant aspects of Rover games was the easy-going atmosphere of the audience compared to the more tense aura surrounding Ranger fans. It was common practice at Rover games for fans to bring balloons, inflate them between periods and then bat them from section to section until they reached the ice and were retrieved by an attendant.

In March 1946, my father took me to another Rangers game. This time the Toronto Maple Leafs—my favorite team—were the opponents, and it loomed like a classic evening. Once again, though, I fell victim to a build-up and letdown. The Leafs had an especially poor club that season—they finished fifth, well out of the playoffs—and in this game appeared supremely indifferent. They lost a three-goal lead and went down to defeat, leaving me crushed and forlorn.

I was now 14 years old and showing a very definite interest in writing. Since 1942, when I was ten, I had been collecting newspaper hockey stories in a scrapbook and writing very biased accounts of the games I saw in the white spaces of the program scorecard.

The major problem was that I could never find enough hockey reading matter to satisfy my thirst; that is, not until September 1946, when I spent one Saturday afternoon at the Paramount Theater in Times Square. Following the show, I walked across 43d Street and discovered an out-of-town newspaper stand. My eyes boggled at the galaxy of papers—St. Louis *Post-Dispatch,* Chicago *Tribune,* St. Paul *Pioneer Press;* on and on until I suddenly noticed *The Globe and Mail* from Toronto. Somehow, I had never expected to find a Canadian paper there. And only five cents more than its regular price! I quickly bought a copy and turned to the sports page.

There, to my astonishment, were not one, not two but *three* hockey stories. I had never imagined there was a newspaper in the *world* that would print more than *two* hockey stories at once. Not only that, but they were good stories and about the Toronto Maple Leafs. I promptly took a subscription and within a week was receiving *The Globe and Mail* delivered daily to my home by the postman. I considered this one of the best bargains I had ever struck.

The Globe and Mail was filled with good writers. At the time Jim Vipond and Al Nickleson covered hockey while Jim Coleman wrote a marvelously witty and often hard-hitting column. On three out of five days, Coleman would write hockey. Fantastic!

Coinciding with my subscription to the *Globe* was the emergence of the Maple Leafs as a new and exciting power

15

in the NHL. All I needed now was a good fan to root for Toronto with me. For some reason, Larry Schildkret's parents were still unwilling to let him attend evening games so I headed for the Rangers-Toronto match that December 1946 with Howie Sparer, my neighbor who really didn't enjoy hockey all that much but tolerated my fanaticism.

However, once the game began my ears were greeted by the sounds of somebody else cheering the Leafs. Better still, he was sitting right next to me. I immediately shook his hand, told him my name and the two of us became fast friends.

Jim Hernon and I were as different as night and day. He was Irish-Catholic, lived in Woodside, Queens—a part of New York I had heard about but never visited—attended a parochial high school and had probably never met a Jew in his life. But our affection for the Maple Leafs first and hockey second was enough to surmount any ethnic or cultural barriers. Jim told me he played roller hockey, as I did, and invited me to come try out for his team, the Woodside Whippets.

He didn't tell me he was the best player on the Whippets, nor that he was one of the finest stickhandlers in the Long Island City YMCA Roller Hockey League. I made that discovery the following Saturday when I took my ball-bearing skates and beat-up Lovell hockey stick out to Woodside and took my audition before the Whippets.

Frankly, I was not all that good and Hernon knew it. But he also knew that his word was enough to get me on the team and he gave his word. "Now," he said, as I skated out to my defense position on the first turn, "all you have to do is pay attention."

"Pay attention" were Jimmy's bywords and, as much as possible, I tried to follow his style. I never was quite as good as he was but I did learn and that winter the Woodside Whippets won the second-place trophy in their league.

In their short, two-year life span, the Whippets won many a thrilling match; and lost a few, too. Whenever we played in the especially tough Astoria section of Queens, Astoria's home team, the Red Wings, would fortify its cheering section with a large contingent of "big guys." When one of us Whippets would be knocked onto the sidewalk he would be "helped" to his feet by several of those spectators but somehow would find himself somewhat bruised about the head by the time he got back into the play.

Since it seems New York City didn't lay out its streets with roller hockey dimensions in mind, several middle-of-the-street rinks were improperly balanced. The Sunnyside Americans (from another section of Queens), for example, played on a court that had the pitch of a ski slope. Very wisely, the Americans managed to skate downhill for two out of the three periods. I vividly recall a game in which the Whippets led the Americans 6-2 in the third period. With ten minutes remaining the Whippets were skating uphill more like tortoises than whippets. The Americans scored three quick goals and I remember that we crowded around our goal net, the victims of an avalanche. Fortunately, Hernon cleared the puck out of danger just when it appeared that the Whippets, net and goalie would be swept down the hill and into the subway station.

Unlike our NHL counterparts, the Whippets did not travel first-class. We used the city bus lines for our more distant games although we had a penchant for talking our way right off the bus. It was not uncommon for one member of the team to shout from the rear of the vehicle, "Does your father work?" Whereupon a teammate would respond, "No, he's a bus driver!" At least twice the Whippets were ordered off the bus following that punch line.

Armed with cowbell and tangerines, Hernon and I religiously attended every Maple Leaf game and soon decided that it would be in the best interests of us both to get

17

season tickets. In this way we would be able to boo the Rangers for 35 games, not just the seven they played against the Maple Leafs.

Rooting against the Rangers was not exactly difficult in those days, since the New York club had suffered terribly from the war. Many of the Rangers returned from the armed forces with their skills dulled beyond repair. But in March 1948 the New Yorkers did reach a playoff berth and, once again, I faced a major conflict.

This time the problem was Passover, the Jewish holiday which is celebrated with a Seder—family services at the evening meal. It had been six years since the Rangers had held a playoff game at the Garden, so the 1948 event was a hockey milestone in New York. The Red Wings of Detroit would be the opposition and I, naturally, had tickets to both New York games. Seder, naturally, was the same night as the first game.

I resolved the problem by attending the first part of services (my Grandmother, who was giving the Seder, thoughtfully moved up the start by about fifteen minutes to accommodate me) and then bolting out with only a smidgen of guilt. Obviously, the hockey deity had it over the Hebrew. There were a few disapproving murmurs heard among aunts and uncles but nothing embarrassing enough to prevent me from doing it again.

Actually, the biggest family vs. hockey crisis occurred the very next day when my cousin Ira came to visit. I had already given Ira, who was eight, his basic training in hockey rooting. He was a Maple Leaf fan through and through, but he also appreciated a good game played by anybody. That night was the second game in the Stanley Cup playoff and I believed it imperative that Ira attend, if only to improve his hockey knowledge. On the afternoon of the match Ira developed a headache severe enough for my grandmother to decide that he shouldn't go to the game.

This was sacrilegious. Of course he would go. But Ira had a thing about not being able to swallow aspirin. How could I cure his headache? I went to the drugstore and got a box of a chewing-gum aspirin, hoping it would work. But Ira spat it out and now we were in trouble. Big trouble.

It was near dinnertime, after which we were to leave. Ira refused to eat and tried a nap. Now *I* was getting sick. At 7 P.M. he awoke and announced that he was ready to go. My grandmother said no, but when I showed her a cushion I had packed to make Ira comfortable, as well as more chewing-gum aspirin and three tangerines, she relented.

For a short time I actually thought Ira would make it. We arrived at the Garden a few minutes before game time and made our way to the upper reaches of the balcony. I arranged the cushion to give him maximum comfort and offered another piece of the chewing gum. This time he took the thing and chewed it for about five minutes by which time the game was in progress.

It was a terribly exciting game; the overpowered Rangers were somehow hanging on for dear life against the Red Wings; something on the order of Ira's ordeal against nausea. Then, midway in the third period he could hold back no more. He wheeled out of his seat and began running up the steps in the direction of the men's room. Just as he reached the top stair he threw up all over the place while a hush fell over the building. The Red Wings had scored and gone ahead to stay. It was the last time Ira ever ate aspirin gum.

By April 1948, my romance with the Maple Leafs had reached its high point. They were clearly the best team in hockey with such marvelous players as Syl Apps, Ted Kennedy, Max Bentley, Turk Broda and "Wild" Bill Ezinicki. They had taken the Stanley Cup in 1947 and again in 1948. I had listened to all the games on my little Philco Transitone. In March 1949, after the Leafs had won

19

their third straight Stanley Cup, my parents bought me a Hallicrafters S-38 short wave radio. My theory was that a short wave set would be much better equipped to receive the broadcasts from Toronto.

I was wrong.

Despite a valiant attempt to erect a short wave antenna from the roof of our brownstone house, I was unable to do any better on the expensive Hallicrafters than on my tiny Philco. Nevertheless, I used the Hallicrafters to listen to the 1950 semi-final round between Toronto and Detroit and blamed the new set for Detroit's victory in the seventh game of the round.

By now I had entered Brooklyn College and begun thinking about a career. In my senior year at high school, I had dreamed of becoming a hockey publicist but could not possibly imagine how this might be translated into reality. As a result I left the "Ambition" part of my yearbook biography blank. Getting a job in hockey was just too much to expect from life.

At the time Brooklyn College did not have hockey but it did have a soccer team and I spent my last two years covering the soccer team for *Kingsman,* the college paper. In my junior year, I worked out an arrangement that gave me Mondays free. It was then I decided to write a newsletter for New York Rovers fans. I took my idea to the Rovers office where Bill Brendle, the Rovers publicist, and Tommy Lockhart, manager of the team, okayed the idea. The newsletter was a two-page mimeographed sheet of Eastern League information which I delivered to the Rovers office every Monday. It was probably the most important step I had taken to get into the hockey business, because through it I met Herb Goren, the Rangers publicity man.

Another break developed at college, of all places. I was meeting with William Pitt, my guidance counselor, and noticed a gold-engraved ashtray on his desk. The engraving mentioned the New York Naval Armed Guard Gunners, a team which had played in the Met League during the war, and one which I had watched many times.

I asked Pitt what his connection was with the Gunners and he said he had been an officer with them and had been close to the hockey team. He said his friend, Stan Saplin, who was then writing hockey for the New York *Journal-American,* had also worked with the Gunners. He asked if I'd like to meet Saplin. It went without saying.

A week later I took the subway to South Street in Manhattan and had my first meeting with a full-fledged hockey writer. When I told Saplin that I wanted to do precisely what he was doing—covering the Rangers for a major daily—he laughed. "Stay out of hockey," he said. "You're wasting your time." I tried to explain how much I disagreed but Saplin was adamant and we parted with a great compatibility of misgivings about each other.

In the meantime my newsletter was winning distinctly minor raves around the Rangers office but was noticed nonetheless, especially by Goren. Each time I brought up another edition we chatted for a minute or two and, by season's end, were reasonably good friends; except that Goren neglected to tell me that the Garden was about to fold the Rovers tent.

I graduated from college that spring of 1954 and planned to go to graduate school in the fall. During the summer I worked at a children's camp and then at an advertising agency in Brooklyn. I fully expected to continue there while earning my M.A. in teaching.

One afternoon early in September I received a phone call from Herb Goren. "How would you like to come to work for the Rangers as my assistant?"

Goren must have wondered at the dead silence that followed. I was desperately trying to digest his words because I was sure this was either part of a dream or a

21

diabolical gag perpetrated by one of my friends. Finally I managed to push the words out: "Of course I would."

"Well," said Goren, deflating the balloon a bit, "I can't say for sure but I have to check with Frank Boucher (the Rangers manager) and find out if any other boys are being considered. In the meantime, just sit tight."

There was no other way to sit. This was precisely the job I had wanted and this was exactly the right time for me to get it. It literally and figuratively was too good to be true; but it wasn't mine for sure yet. I decided I would simply keep my mouth shut about Goren's offer until it connected or fell through. The next twenty hours are among the longest I can remember.

Goren called back at 4 P. M. the next day.

"You'll start next week, if you want the job," he said. "We'll pay you $50 a week and all the hockey games you can watch. What do you think?"

My mind had already raced halfway to the Garden.

"What do I think? What do *you* think I think? I'll be in your office the first thing tomorrow!"

I had only one misgiving. If I was going to work for the Rangers, how could I possibly root for the Maple Leafs?

It was a silly question. I was now a Ranger fan!

II

LIFE IN
THE PROPAGANDA
MINISTRY

A press agent for a hockey club is no different from a propaganda minister for the Pentagon. The "facts" he offers range from exaggerations of the truth to outright lies, depending on the occasion. Sometimes the lies are modest and thus quite acceptable to the reporters—and public—to whom they are dispensed.

Attendance figures fall under the apron of modest lies. No hockey press agent is privy to attendance figures while a game is in progress since it takes time for the arena to compile these figures. But since newspapermen feel compelled to proclaim some arithmetic in their stories, the press agents always oblige.

They do so by scanning the crowd, estimating how many thousand people they can add to what appears to be the correct total and balancing that with what they think their club owners would like to see in the papers. Inevitably their attendance figures are at least 1,000-2,000 above the correct figure. When they go higher, the reporters often feel obliged to comment. ("The crowd was announced as 13,000; which means that 6,000 fans were disguised as seats.")

Immodest lies are generally linked to injuries. A star player will get hurt—break an ankle or tear knee ligaments—but the club will decide it would rather not have the world know about it. The club press agent will then describe the injury to the reporters as no injury at all, or in absurdly mild terms, suggesting for instance that the star will probably miss a couple of games because of flu.

When I went to work for the Rangers in September 1954, I was immediately pressed into telling modest lies. This had to do with writing personality blurbs about the players for the program and for the press and radio guide—both edited by my boss, Herb Goren.

Goren was known as "Herbie" or "The Old Scout," depending on how long you'd known him. Recent acquaintances called him Herbie because they didn't know that as a crackerjack young sportswriter for the old *New York Sun,* he had taken over a venerable staff-written column called "The Old Scout." He'd done it so well that he owned the pillar of piffle (as newsmen call such columns) until the *Sun* folded. Hence, those who remembered Herbie from 'way back when always called him Scout; he always seemed to brighten a little when that happened.

I will be forever indebted to Goren for hiring me. I learned more from him just by watching than I did from almost anyone else in the newspaper or writing business. The first thing I learned was that it was physically possible for a man's fingers to strike typewriter keys six times faster than mine were at the time, *and* make sense while doing it. (And I thought I was typing fast!) The speed with which Goren could knock out a press release or a story—he frequently did freelance assignments too, but we'll get to that—was nerve-racking, if not plain awesome.

The second thing I learned was to ask questions, because twelve times out of thirteen Goren would not volunteer any tips of the trade. He just didn't have time between his work for the Rangers and his outside jobs. (Phil Watson, who later became Rangers coach, once described the situation thus: "I took care of the publicity while Goren, the publicity man, wrote articles for *The Police Gazette.*")

The third thing I learned, and the one which did me the most good later, was to service the media hand and foot. If, as often happened, Howard Cosell stalked into the office and demanded ten good questions for his radio show, I quickly produced ten questions for him. If Stan Saplin (my pessimistic friend from the *Journal-American*) wanted the names of Detroit's high-scoring line of 1936, he got the answer in a matter of minutes. No request was too difficult for our department, as long as I handled it and let Herbie do his outside work.

Which is neither a complaint nor a knock at Herbie since in many ways, he was an excellent publicity man. The Scout's forte was an amazing rapport with the sportswriters, no matter how cranky they were (Dana Mozley of the *Daily News*), no matter how outrageous their copy (Jim Burchard of the *World-Telegram and Sun*), no matter how critical they were of the Rangers (Stan Saplin of the *Journal-American*). The reporters respected Goren because only a few years earlier he had been one of them and he, in turn, was properly sensitive to their needs. In fact, from time to time he would even ghostwrite hockey pieces for some of the reporters.

I felt an excellent rapport with Goren; something akin to a warmth one might experience for a likeable but eccentric older brother. After all, we had a lot in common. We both were Jewish which was unusual in the hockey scene; both from modest Brooklyn families; both had inexhaustible drive and, best of all, we both loved hockey. Since Goren had been through the professional writing mill already, he had learned to temper his enthusiasm, especially his rooting interest in the Rangers. "The one thing you don't do in the

25

press box," he warned me before opening night, "is root. That's out!"

Well, it *was* out until opening night when I couldn't help noticing Goren leaning over the edge of the mezzanine press box, screaming for the referee's scalp.

As press agents went, Goren was also respected for his conservatism. Although attendance figures were always fictional, he made a point of underestimating rather than overestimating the crowds. "This way," he'd say, "the guys will believe me on more important stories."

The "more important stories" were those Herbie hoped to plant in the dull days of February and March when the Rangers figured to be mired in fifth or sixth place, clearly out of playoff contention. You see, the only negative aspect of my wonderful job was the abject mediocrity of the Rangers. They were, to be kind about the whole thing, a lousy hockey club.

This was obvious since they had not reached the playoffs for four straight years and seemed unlikely to do so in this, the 1954-55 season. Their leading scorer was a chap named Danny Lewicki, who could skate like the wind and shoot the puck just as hard as you could want—as long as there weren't any opponents within fifteen feet. Their second leading scorer, Andy Bathgate, finished so far down the scoring list you needed a magnifying glass to locate his name. Their defense had a sprinkling of rookies and one marvelous man named Ivan Irwin, appropriately dubbed by Goren, "Ivan the Terrible." We never were quite sure whether the nickname applied to his fearsome character or his playing ability.

Irwin actually was an eminently likeable character who did not skate too well but was terrifically strong and loved to take on the biggest men and highest scorers on the other side. He was Goren's favorite subject; and deservedly so.

Our home opener in 1954 was on a Wednesday night,

against the Boston Bruins, a better club than the Rangers but one we believed was catchable, as opposed to the mighty Detroit Red Wings and Montreal Canadiens. To help the Rangers win, I decided to punish myself in hopes of working some reverse magic: I ate dinner in a seedy cafeteria across from Madison Square Garden "for good luck."

To my astonishment, not to mention Goren's, the Rangers won the game. Which meant that on Sunday, before the second home game, I had to eat there again. Sorrowfully, I discovered that the roast beef sandwich, awful though it had been, was not on the Sunday menu. Should I turn and leave or should I go with the cafeteria's magic and another dish. I decided on franks and beans this time. Again the Rangers won.

By now, I was convinced of the effectiveness of the magic but terribly worried about dysentery. In a way I was hoping the Rangers would lose the following Wednesday so I could get out of the cafeteria syndrome. This time the Rangers cooperated.

The quality, or lack of it, of the team was a handicap to Goren and me but we were helped on the other hand by the warmth and easy accessibility of Frank Boucher, the manager, whom Goren correctly described as one of the two nicest men in the world. (The other being columnist Frank Graham.)

Boucher was an exceptionally tender gentleman with an affection for music—he did a splendid song-and-dance routine with Joe Nichols of *The New York Times* to the tune of "Are You From Dixie?"—and good fellowship. To a man, the press corps respected Boucher as a person although Saplin frequently expressed doubt about his managerial ability. As a result the newspapermen tended to be kinder to the Rangers than they might have been if the club had been managed by a lesser man.

The coach was huge Murray ("Muzz") Patrick, former

heavyweight boxing champion of Canada, former Ranger defenseman and son of the famed Lester "Silver Fox" Patrick, who set up the first Ranger team in Madison Square Garden. Muzz was something of a blunderbuss but a rather lovable one. In the dressing room and on the bench he was a commanding figure because of his size, not to mention his penetrating voice which frequently convinced the normally unconvincible types among the Fourth Estate.

Muzz managed to keep the team above water through mid-November when the Bruins returned to New York for their traditional Thanksgiving Eve game against the Rangers. The day before the game, I participated in my first major news story as assistant publicist. The Rangers traded their first-rate defenseman Al Stanley and a forward named Nick Mickoski to Chicago for Bill Gadsby, an accomplished defenseman, and Pete Conacher, the son of the great Charlie Conacher of the Toronto Maple Leafs.

From all appearances it looked like the deal that would finally catapult the Rangers into the playoffs. Stanley had been too unobtrusive a defenseman to suit the bash-oriented New York fans. Time after time the spectators would jeer the big fellow, calling him "Sonja" and other less printable names. Boucher's trade was an act of mercy for Stanley. Mickoski was one of those big, affectionate Li'l Abner types who just couldn't put the puck into the net often enough. We would miss him but Conacher was younger and supposedly a more effective shooter.

Both the newcomers played marvelously inspired hockey in their New York début against Boston. The Rangers won handily and all signs were pointing to the playoffs, except there was one mishap. Late in the game Gadsby thrust his head in front of a Bruin shot. This act of courage was rewarded with one badly broken beak and Gadsby would be out of action indefinitely.

Of course we didn't know it at the time but the exultation of Thanksgiving Eve was to be the last either Herb,

Boucher, Patrick or I would experience for the rest of the season. Gadsby was gone and Conacher turned out to be a bust. The rest of the team was sub-mediocre and didn't win a single game throughout December. Christmas was so bad that even the famous homemade egg nog annually concocted by Sam B. Gunst, an old friend of Goren's, was so rank Herbie had to pour it down the drain as soon as Sam left the office.

The defeats, depressing though they were, never once dulled my love of the job nor my excitement in the game. I religiously attended every practice held at the rink on the top floor of the Garden and was perhaps too gung-ho to suit some of the more cynical newsmen.

One of them told me about Carl Shatto, a hockey writer who covered the Cleveland Barons of the American Hockey League, at that time the leading minor league in the country, just under the NHL. Shatto was once involved in a poker match with a few other reporters in the clubhouse when a young writer burst in to announce that the team was on the ice. "Aren't you coming out to watch the practice?" asked the eager, young reporter.

The venerable Shatto calmly shuffled the deck and replied: "Why, have they found a new way to practice?"

Another newsman who gave me various insights was Howard Cosell, who had recently given up his law practice to concentrate on radio. It was obvious from the manner in which he analyzed my questions that he was several cuts above the traditional sports reporter.

"In the jock approach to journalism," Cosell explained, "every play is the greatest, every athlete is always giving it the old 110 per cent, every owner is dedicated to the public good. People today don't buy that stuff anymore. They want announcers searching for the truth."

I applauded Cosell but felt deep down that he was a good ten years ahead of his time.

Cosell was the exception. Several of the reporters on the

29

beat started me on the road to disillusionment before the season was half over. One of them was Jim Burchard of the *World-Telegram.* Known to the players as "Thirsty Jim," Burchard was a huge, wild-living type who dominated any scene he happened to enter. His voice was mighty and his laughter, once it got going, sounded like the starting mechanism on Jack Benny's Maxwell.

Burchard was a marvelous storyteller whose affection for one-eighth truths seemed to be a direct rip-off of W.C. Fields. And, naturally, he liked to drink. He also liked to twit Boucher and Patrick, although his affection for hockey was deep. Yet, as much as he liked the game, Burchard treated his job the way an athletic-minded youngster regards homework. The less study involved, the happier he would be.

One evening a few minutes before game time, Burchard climbed down to the press box, his broad-brimmed black fedora turned down both front and back in traditional fashion, and handed me a package of envelopes, each with the NHL imprimatur in one corner. I knew immediately that this was the packet for his All-Star votes. "Here, kid," said Burchard, "fill these out for me!"

I couldn't believe my ears. What could be more important to a hockey writer than selecting the All-Star Team. Naturally, I was honored that Burchard allowed me to make his picks but I found it hard to believe that he took such a light view of the matter.

Anyway, having suffered through December without a win and with little hope for the next three months, the Rangers for all intents and purposes were eliminated from the playoffs by mid-season. This made the job of publicist more than difficult; it was virtually impossible. What we needed, of course, was a new face in the lineup; somebody who would provide copy for the hungry newsmen, and inspiration for Goren. Boucher finally imported Lou Fontinato, a truculent young defenseman from the Rangers farm team in Vancouver.

As in the case of the chicken and the egg, it's impossible to determine whether Goren "made" Fontinato a New York—and later an NHL—personality or whether Louie owned all the ingredients to begin with and Goren mined them and refined them into headlines. In any event Louie had star quality. He was husky, raw-boned, naturally tough and, most important, colorful.

When the referee sentenced him to the penalty box, Louie would become so peeved over the call he would jump a foot or two up in the air in Latin disgust. (Goren liked to claim that he first encouraged Louie to do his jump.) Immediately Goren tagged him "Leapin' Louie"; he was also known as "Louis The Leaper," depending on the newspaper space available at the time.

Despite the Rangers' low estate, Louie's lust for combat was so great that New York hockey fans took to him as if he were the redeemer. Goren realized that it was only a matter of time before the non-hockey writers discovered Fontinato. (Goren was extremely friendly with Red Smith and Frank Graham, two of the city's most respected sports columnists but they rarely wrote about hockey.) When Fontinato had established himself, Goren put through a call to Red Smith and the Tribune's ace showed up at just the right time; a game between the Rangers and the Montreal Canadiens. Goren's judgement was rewarded on two counts—it was a wildly exciting game, and Smith wrote a marvelous column about it:

"In a sense it was to be a small circus of the Roman type, starring Lou Fontinato, the Wild Man of Guelph, Ont., in gladiatorial combat with Maurice Richard, the Rocket of Mount Royal . . .

"The Rangers' dark defenseman is no admirer of the Marquis of Queensberry. Strictly a London Prize Ring

31

man, he had his padded gloves off in the fragment of an instant. A lovely right caught Richard just outside the left eye. Skin burst and flesh cracked and blood ran in little parallel trickles down the Rocket's face, staining his white shirt . . . Pure joy swept the galleries."

Fontinato was the answer to Goren's prayers, but he had come too late to redeem the season. He played in twenty-eight games for the Rangers who were obligated to ship him back to Vancouver whence he would return the following year and become a New York standby. With the final two months to go and even fourth place out of sight, another hunk of good copy was needed. And another player.

The player Boucher had in mind was Bill "Wild Bill" Ezinicki, who had terrorized the Rangers as a star for the Maple Leafs and later the Bruins, but was now approaching the end of his career skating for Vancouver in the minors. Still Ezinicki was known to New Yorkers and carried the mantle of toughness so desirable to the Ranger team.

The night Boucher put in the call to Vancouver for him, "Wild Bill" was out on the ice, breaking his thumb in a vicious fist fight. It was a big disappointment for Goren who had plans for promoting Ezinicki and it was a crusher to me because "Wild Bill" had been one of my favorites when I was rooting for the Maple Leafs.

Ezinicki's arrival was delayed as the Rangers continued to lose. Finally, in desperation, Boucher decided to bring in "Wild Bill" anyway, although the broken thumb had not healed; he would wear a protective guard and play with his thumb in a cast.

Having watched Ezinicki carefully for years, I regarded myself as the country's leading expert on his moves and mannerisms. I vowed to do everything possible to trumpet his presence and the moment Ezinicki arrived I went to work. Goren did, too, and between us we obtained about five times as much space as "Wild Bill" warranted, although we didn't realize it at the time.

Ezinicki's first Ranger game was greeted with a larger than normal crowd, although his performance was hardly exceptional. He was, as usual, pleasantly disputatious and the fans looked forward to the night when Montreal would return and "Wild Bill" would face one of his old adversaries, Maurice "Rocket" Richard.

In the meantime, I had work to do. I was determined to plant more Ezinicki stories. That Monday afternoon, Dana Mozley of the *Daily News* dropped in to the office looking for an off-day feature. For some reason Goren wasn't around so I suggested that he do a piece on Ezinicki. "What can I write?" said Mozley, "Ezinicki isn't here."

Although I hadn't, I told Mozley that I had just talked with "Wild Bill" and he had carefully explained to me his three varieties of bodychecks—The Jolt, The Thump and The Whomp. The Jolt was his mild one, it simply threw an opponent off balance; The Thump was more devastating while The Whomp either would knock a man unconscious or deposit him in the seats.

My private justification for the fib was that these *were* Ezinicki's three types of bodychecks, it was just that nobody ever had gotten around to putting them down in proper literary form. Mozley seemed very impressed, thanked me and went back to his office. After he left, I went down to the Ranger dressing room to get some equipment for an exhibit, when who do I meet but "Wild Bill" himself.

Judging by the size of the goose pimples on my arms, I might as well have been meeting God. I introduced myself to Ezinicki as calmly as possible under the circumstances and he responded casually. I then informed him I was trying to do as much as possible to publicize his arrival with the Rangers.

"I wouldn't overdo that if I were you," he said while standing in front of the dressing room urinal, "after all, I'm not in such good shape."

Then I told him about the Jolt, Thump and Whomp. From his expression, I couldn't be sure if he was just plain disgusted or despairing. This much was certain; he was not at all happy. I hung my head, apologized and walked back to Goren's office, still convinced that I had done the right thing.

The story appeared for what it was worth, but Ezinicki was indeed *not* in good shape and in 16 games did virtually nothing for the Rangers. When he skated against the Detroit Red Wings and his old arch-foe, Ted Lindsay, "Wild Bill" was nothing but Sweet William. In the well-touted confrontation with Rocket Richard, Ezzie came closest to making the big hit we had been waiting for.

It was midway in the second period when Richard took a pass near center ice and began gathering speed for a rush along his right wing. Ezinicki had a habit of skating aimlessly up the other side of the rink when suddenly he would swing into orbit and, like a guided missile, would come crashing violently into his target.

As Richard sped over the center red line, Ezinicki swerved sharply to his left and described a wide arc as he crossed the rink on collision course with The Rocket. By the time "Wild Bill" was fifteen feet from Richard it appeared to the 13,000 spectators that The Rocket's career was about to come to an abrupt and hideous end.

What everyone, including me, had overlooked was the fact that Richard had played against Ezinicki for almost a decade. A split-second before the anticipated moment of impact, Richard lunged to the left, like a driver going around a double-parked car, and continued goalward as if nothing had happened. And, naturally, nothing did happen. Ezinicki made contact with the air and little else and all

Ranger fans could do was muse about what might have been. It was the closest that "Wild Bill" ever came to achieving glory in a Ranger uniform.

As the final weeks of the season approached, I became more and more uneasy since I knew I would be dismissed as soon as the season was over; and I was convinced there was not another job in the world I could tolerate after being so deeply involved with hockey. What's more, Goren and Boucher had been complimentary to the point of giving me an unexpected raise from $50 to $55 in mid-season. That made me want to stay too.

Two weeks before the final game Goren took me aside and mentioned that time was running out. I knew *that;* what mattered was whether or not I'd be back the following season. He assured me that if *he* returned, I would return—but in the meantime, I'd better go out and find a job. He also said my going-away present would be a free trip to Montreal for the playoffs.

That was a dandy gift. Tha Rangers finished in fifth place, fifteen points out of the nearest playoff berth and nine points out of the cellar. The Canadiens went all the way to the finals and I "camped" in the NHL press suite. When the last writer had departed for the night, I hopped into bed and was up the next morning before the first newspaperman arrived. It was a marvelous source of contacts. I got to really know some terrific reporters I had only encountered during my tenure with the Rangers. More than ever, I felt there was only one world in which to live and that was the hockey world.

Which explains why I suffered a terrible culture shock on returing home. It was mid-April, the season was over and I had to find work. To my dismay, Goren was no help at all. The best he could do was send me over to Seymour Sywoff at the Al Munro Elias Baseball Bureau on 42d Street where I pored over box scores for two days before handing in my resignation. I finally wound up with a job as assistant editor of *International Projectionist,* a film trade magazine which didn't interest me at all but did provide a weekly paycheck and a smidgen of experience in magazine publishing.

I also managed to obtain part-time work with the Long Island daily *Press,* handling schoolboy sports. I was enroute to the *Press* one afternoon on the subway when I peered over a man's shoulder to read a headline that gave me shock: *"RANGERS FIRE FRANK BOUCHER; MUZZ PATRICK NAMED SUCCESSOR."*

Much as I wanted to, I couldn't quite break down and cry. Instead, I spent the next six hours with a sick-to-my-stomach feeling that just wouldn't go away. I tried to phone Goren but couldn't get through and finally decided to visit the office the following day, more or less to confirm what I hoped really hadn't happened, knowing full well that it had.

I prayed Boucher wouldn't be there but he was. Throughout the season, no matter how sadly weak his Rangers were, Boucher somehow managed to give off a ray of goodness; or was it happiness? This time he looked like a corpse. He could barely lift his head in greeting and I could barely muster words of condolence. Patrick had already moved into the manager's office. I left as soon as possible. It isn't easy losing a second father.

Goren later assured me that *he* would remain although he was as furious with the firing as anyone. He said that he would contact me in late August so we could make plans for my return immediately after Labor Day. I couldn't wait.

Early in August, while moping through another day at *International Projectionist,* I received a call from my friend Jack Zanger, an editor at *Sport* magazine. He wondered whether I would like to work for a newspaper, the *Journal-American* to be precise. "Max Kase (sports editor of the newspaper) has offered me the job," said Zanger, "but I don't want to leave *Sport.* I'm recommending you."

I didn't want the job, hoping still to go back with the Rangers, but I couldn't afford not to go through the motions. I told Zanger I was interested. He spelled out the details: Stan Saplin was quitting the *Journal-American* sports staff and would be replaced by Dave Anderson, who had been writing sports for the Brooklyn Section of the paper. I would take Anderson's old Brooklyn beat. Saplin—the man who had once told me to stay out of hockey—had also recommended me.

I made an appointment to see Max Kase. By that time I must have wanted the job after all. I'd been doing a few freelance pieces, and I brought along a set of clippings, including my interview with Alex Webster, who had just come down to play for the football Giants. Kase introduced me to John W. Newton, editor of the Brooklyn Section. While not totally impressed with me—I later learned that was a typical Newtonian facade—Newton agreed I should be hired.

All of a sudden I decided I *didn't* want the job again!

I couldn't imagine myself writing about anything but hockey. Hockey was all that mattered and the other stuff—baseball, football, basketball—was for Philistines. I phoned Goren and told him I had to meet him immediately.

We had lunch at the Automat Cafeteria across the street from Grand Central Terminal. I explained about the offer and told him I didn't want to leave hockey. This time there was no concealing the tears.

Goren was rarely moved by anything and I'm not sure he was touched this time but he was earnest and sensitive and he told me straight out there was no way that I could rationalize refusing the *Journal-American* offer. "Take it," he insisted. "You'll have plenty of time to write hockey on the side. This could be the big step for you in the newspaper business."

A week later I wrote my first column for the New York *Journal-American*.

III

AT WAR WITH THE RANGERS—ROUND ONE, FISCHLER vs. WATSON

Of all the characters I've covered in more than seventeen years in hockey, none inspired a more intense love-hate relationship than Phil Watson, who became coach of the Rangers in September 1955, the year I became Brooklyn sports columnist for the New York *Journal-American.* My work there rarely involved the Rangers, but I managed to become the New York correspondent for *The Hockey News,* a weekly published by Ken McKenzie in Montreal, who also brought out the monthly *Hockey Pictorial.* McKenzie, a large, overbearing backslapper, broke in as publicity director of the NHL in 1946 and soon began publishing the weekly that emerged as the official-unofficial organ of the sport.

The Hockey News usually ran two stories a week on the Rangers. Since it was the only publication in the business it was regarded as something more than a bible to players, coaches, managers and fans alike; particularly in New York where hockey coverage was always skimpy. So my columns became acutely important to Watson who was extremely anxious to make good in his rookie season as an NHL coach.

38

As a personality, Watson was a prize. He was born in Canada, of a Scotch father and a French-Canadian mother, and his temperament was highly volatile. It was not uncommon for Watson, as a star center for the Rangers, to burst into tears at critical moments of play. He was handsome in a sinister, George Raftish sort of way: brown hair parted in the middle, alert green eyes and a synthetic smile; synthetic because he wore a four-tooth bridge as a result of assorted sticks in the mouth received in the gentle sport of hockey.

"They tell me lightning don't strike twice in the same place," Watson liked to say with a rueful, French-Canadian snicker, "but I know better. I been hit, not twice and not three times, more like a hunnert, some places."

Watson's ability—or inability, as the case may be—to stickhandle the English language appealed to newsmen who always seemed to be on the trail of morsels of humor. One night Watson became highly indignant at the foul play of a veteran defenseman on the other team. "McDonald," Watson shouted, "you're nothing but a *BEEN-HAS!*"

Only Watson failed to discern the humor in his outburst. But his funnybone was tickled another night when he was relating an anecdote to Lew Burton, a sportswriter, in the Rangers dressing room after a game which had featured a really spectacular brawl between Watson and the Detroit Red Wings.

Burton interrupted to ask, "How'd it get started, Phil?"

Watson jumped up and cried, "I tell you, Lew, they started it like this!" and brought a hockey stick crashing down on Burton's head, benching him for about twenty minutes. "It was the wrong way to tell that story," Watson would relate with a Gallic grin.

During calm moments, Watson's English was somewhat to the left of impeccable. But when the adrenalin began flowing he'd fall into a mongrel jargon including bits of

French and many curiously garbled Americanisms as well as other material of no traceable root.

"Pollution!" he would shout. "I run you up two trees, you no-brains, *mal de tête,* mother of pig, been-has, *fils de chien!"*

I received my first introduction to Watson's polyglot wrath early in his maiden season. Actually, Watson did have one previous coaching stint in the NHL to his credit. During a home game of the 1940-41 season, the Rangers' coach, Frank Boucher, was out of town on a scouting trip and Watson was deputized to pilot the team. He led his charges to an exciting 5-3 defeat by getting involved in five fights, for three of which he received penalties totaling roughly one-third of the game. "The job sort of went to his head," Boucher said later. "Phil apparently figured to win by sending the entire opposition out on stretchers."

The coaching job in 1955-56 also went to his head but, this time, Watson was a winner. He inherited a flock of young players who were just ripening. Skaters such as Andy Bathgate (doing much better than he had the previous year), Harry Howell, Dean Prentice, Lou Fontinato and Ron Murphy suddenly turned the once floundering Rangers into Stanley Cup-contenders. Watson's chief contribution to the team was his hot-headed urge to win, which he transmitted to the players and the writers.

As much as I enjoyed Watson for his obvious color, I found other aspects of his personality hard to digest. He seemed to relish a put-down, especially if he was inflicting it on someone incapable of fighting back. Phil's voice would climb an octave, the decibels rose and his features seemed arranged in the permanent statement "You're a liar!"

He frightened me, a new kid on the beat who was more awed by the invigorating scene than critical. Besides, who could be critical? Watson alternately shouted, coaxed and cajoled his team into third-place, the highest Rangers standing since the beginning of World War II. He had become a hero on and off Broadway.

Privately, I was irked by Watson's tactics. When the Montreal Canadiens came to town Phil devised a Machiavellian scheme for disrupting their gifted young center, Jean Beliveau. Watson suggested that several writers phone Beliveau on the afternoon of the game, requesting interviews. Although players usually spend the afternoon hours getting some sleep, the gracious Beliveau tired himself out answering questions for newsmen. He was of no value that night in the game and Watson's habitual expression of resigned defiance curled into a broad, satisfied grin while his alert green eyes were wider than ever.

More than anything I resented the fact that Watson was riding the crest of a wave whose energy was provided by Boucher. Without the Bathgates and Fontinatos groomed by Boucher, Watson would have been impotent as a coach. But Phil not only never acknowledged Boucher's contribution, he even twitted his former mentor. Watson felt that he alone was responsible for the Rangers success.

It didn't take long for the flaws to appear in Watson's armor. Too often he treated his major league skaters as if they were amateur peewees. He was especially harsh on goalie Lorne "Gump" Worsley, a normally jolly chap whenever Watson wasn't around. "Worsley is not a mature man," Watson told reporters one day. "He gets away with murder because the fans don't get on him. They like a small, crewcut, cute goalie. You praise the guy and he'll let you down."

Soon, the players rebelled, and early in the 1956-57 season hate began to bubble forth in the Rangers dressing room. Watson began taunting Bronco Horvath, a hawknosed center with a lighthearted attitude. One morning Watson shouted, "Bronco, why in hell aren't you scoring?" Horvath, displaying a kind of instinctive legal ingenuity,

41

detected the loophole in Watson's question and replied: "Coach, it's kind of tough scoring from the end of the bench!"

Horvath was traded and, in 1959-60, was runner-up in the scoring championship. It was the first of innumerable Watsonian blunders.

Until the early part of the 1956-57 season the sportswriters covering the Rangers had treated Watson with fatherly tolerance. But now some were becoming less patient with him, particularly since Watson had blown his top *at them*. At first Watson would acknowledge, with a look of bitter self-reproach, that he got worked up too often and too violently. He'd blame his Latin blood, implying it was an aspect of his nature for which he was not responsibile and which he could not be expected to control. "All the French act like that," he would say. "They're a mighty strange bunch."

Despite Phil's eruptions, his scathing indictments of Worsley, Horvath and anyone else he might have in mind—one day he said to Howie Maurer of the Long Island *Press* and me, "These Rangers are gutless, chicken and print it!"—the Rangers bobbed along on a relatively smooth sea of wins and ties with only an occasional disrupting defeat. On October 24, 1956 the Rangers defeated the powerful Canadiens 3-2 at Madison Square Garden and looked like a solid second-place team. They had won four games, lost two and tied one. What's more they had a favorable schedule ahead and appeared to be resigned to Watson's erratic behavior.

On the evening of October 28th, the Rangers were host to the Toronto Maple Leafs, clearly the second-worst team in the NHL, the worst being Chicago's Black Hawks. New York nursed a 1-0 lead for most of the contest but somehow managed to allow the Canadian sextet to tie the score late in the third period. The game ended in a 1-1 draw, which was something less than a tragedy to everyone but Watson. He huffed and puffed around the coach's room like a steam locomotive, virtually daring reporters to question him.

The newsmen tried to calm Watson with a few sedative observations on the folly of getting upset by a 1-1 tie, but that line of reasoning was ineffectual. There were ominous suggestions in his critique of the team, and they were spelled out the following day when he appeared at the weekly hockey writers luncheon in Leone's Restaurant.

Watson astonished the audience with the announcement that he had dispatched several of his more accomplished players—including Camille Henry and Ron Murphy, to the Providence farm team in the American League.

"Better to take action now," Watson explained, "than after we lose six straight."

After a season of writing saccharine-filled stories about the Rangers, I took my first step into the no-man's-land of criticism. Knowing Watson's boiling point, I vaguely understood that I was treading on thin ice and that one negative sentence about his coaching would have long-term reverberations. But my cerebral tug-of-war was no contest. I *had* to write what I believed, and I believed that Watson was being suckered by his emotions; that it was downright absurd to demote such accomplished players to the minors. This is precisely what I wrote, heretic as it may have seemed to Watson.

The story was mailed to *The Hockey News* on a Monday and appeared in print the following weekend. By that time the Rangers had lost 7-2 to Toronto and 4-1 to Boston. The hockey writers convened at Leone's again for a luncheon on the afternoon following the Boston defeat. Watson's pique was obvious from the moment he walked in. He sat at the head table, flanked by general manager Muzz Patrick and my old boss, publicist Herb Goren. Watson was doing a slow burn. He bit his lip, frequently stared off into space and said nothing—at least not until the time had come for the coach's weekly report.

Watson began his defense by spitting a long series of adjectives and verbs at the writers and concluded with a classic display of his omission of the "t" at the end of a key word. "Our bubble," he shouted, "has not *burss!*"

He did not direct any of his invective toward me personally, but I nevertheless had considerable trouble eating my beloved shrimp with Leone's special cream sauce. My heart was beating a paradiddle in anticipation of what, if anything, Watson would do or say to me. Having assured us that the Rangers bubble had not burst, the coach suddenly put every writer in the audience on the defensive.

He started with the newspaperman closest to his seat and pointed an accusing finger at Al Laney of the *Herald-Tribune*. "You, Al," snapped Watson, "which one of dose guys dat I sent down would you've kept on de Rangers?" Realizing that he wasn't expected to answer, Laney said nothing. Watson got the signal and proceeded to the next writer as if he was the prosecuting attorney addressing each member of the jury. The next was Howie Maurer of the Long Island *Press*. "What about you, Howie—who would you've kept?" No reply. Then, Jim Burchard of the *World-Telegram and Sun*. No answer. Dave Anderson of the *Journal-American*. Silence.

Until this point Watson had proceeded in order. Now, he had reached my seat. My left foot was feverishly moving up and down like a driver futilely pumping the brakes on a car gone out of control. But Watson passed me by deliberately. "What about you Dana?" he half-shouted at Dana Mozley of the *Daily News*. Like the others, Mozley said nothing.

By now I couldn't decide whether I wanted Watson to overlook me or not. Whatever happened would be embarrassing. At last Watson had come to the end of the line. His voice had carefully developed a crescendo as he orchestrated his finale. Suddenly, however, the shout abated and he carefully transformed his tone to a cool snarl. I could almost taste the venom on his lips as he said, "And you, Fischler, who would *you* have kept on the Rangers?"

It was the moment of truth and I knew it. To remain silent was to confirm Watson's decision and cool the flames of passion. Still, I wanted to say something, but I had to somehow figure out a way to crank out the words.

There was a silence of approximately three seconds—although it seemed like thirty—until I managed to blurt, "I would have kept Camille Henry and Ron Murphy!"

Watson was stunned to the core. Apparently, he had never expected a reply and therefore was unprepared for my simple assertion. Then, he blew his cool and nearly shook the foundations of the restaurant.

"Well, dat convinces me you know nutting about 'ockey!!"

I wanted to dive under the table and crawl out of Leone's via the kitchen door. Instead, I sat mummified by Watson's explosion. The roar ended the luncheon rather abruptly, and I realized, then and there that, like it or not, I had gone to war with the Establishment.

Whether I would have done it all over again, knowing the consequences, remains a question. I was branded a rebel then and there, and the physical and mental strain have been difficult to absorb through the years. On the other hand there was immense satisfaction in feeling I had done the right thing, if only because I genuinely believed that it was right.

The immediate consequences of the confrontation were fear of reprisal from Watson and Patrick and a terrific bout of constipation that remained with me until the end of the season. If nothing else, I prayed that my appraisal of the Rangers would turn out right. Inevitably, I began rooting for them to lose. And they obliged. Boston 4, New York 2. Montreal 4, New York 2. Detroit 6, New York 4. Montreal 5, New York 3! When Watson dispatched the players to Providence, he had insisted, "Better now than to lose six straight." The 5-3 loss to Montreal was the Rangers sixth straight defeat.

Another luncheon was held following the sixth loss. I wondered just how Watson would behave under the circumstances. I suspected he would cross us up and maintain decorum. I was wrong. He was as bellicose as ever, but, for some reason—perhaps my breakthrough the previous week—the writers were less awed by Watson. He demanded once again that he had made the right moves, blasted me once more and concluded, "Why even General Motors can make a mistake."

I was about to insert a retort at this point when, to my amazement, another writer popped up. "Yea, Phil," he said, "but General Motors never lost six straight!" The brave gentleman was Paul Durkin, a delightful, buck-toothed writer for the Newark *Star-Ledger*. His squelch was too perfect for Watson to handle, but Durkin wasn't through with the coach. He returned to his newspaper and wrote a lengthy column supporting my position while putting down Watson's behavior as "small potatoes." Any doubts I may have had about my behavior were erased when I read Durkin's column.

Better still, several of the Rangers came to my support. Camille Henry, the will 'o the wisp left wing, (whom the typically erratic Watson had since called *back* from Providence) and Andy Bathgate, the club's leading scorer, both urged me to remain steadfast and suggested that my criticism was well-taken. "Screw Watson!" was the theme.

I didn't have to; Watson was screwing himself with his frenzied handling of the team. The Rangers responded by refusing to win a hockey game. In fact the club did not win a game from October 25th through November 21st and I never looked better. What's more, I discovered that people were reading me and responding to my criticism much more readily than to the weekly saccharine I had previously dispensed.

The Leone's episode permanently liberated me from the Establishment, although years passed before I realized the significance of the incident. Once freed, new writing vistas immediately opened to me. I contacted Ken McKenzie, my publisher on *The Hockey News* and suggested a profile on Watson for his monthly *Pictorial*.

"This one will be different," I insisted, "a deep, psychological look at this wild man." McKenzie, who as my pieces in both his publications became tougher was to develop into one of the most timid publishers alive, agreed. The article was succinct but solid. My angle was apparent: Watson was hockey's answer to Eddie Stanky, the second baseman-turned-manager of the St. Louis Cardinals. In Stanky's first two years as manager, the Cardinals finished third. In his third season (1954) St. Louis was sixth and Stanky was fired. Both Watson and Stanky were volatile, overemotional types, likely to antagonize their own players as well as the foe.

The article was as fair as I could make it. Watson's assets were spelled out, but there were enough negative parts to make it clear that he was not my choice for man of the year. A statement by one of the players' friends apparently angered Watson more than anything. It went this way:

"Watson lost [contact with] his men toward the end of last season. At the start, they feared and respected him, but his constant threats, quotes and digs in the paper were overdone. He hardly praised his guys and they, in turn, won't play [their best] for him unless he changes his ways and treats the players as adults. Oh yea, he may get 'em into the playoffs, but another coach might get 'em even higher than second, third or fourth.''

In conclusion I pointed out that Stanky never changed his style and wound up in the minors. I made it clear that unless Watson changed his ways, he would be bounced out of New York.

Written late in November, the article did not appear until the January 1957 issue of *Hockey Pictorial*. By then my relations with Watson had stabilized to a point where we tolerated if not loved each other. The appearance of *Hockey Pictorial* in January did for Watson and me what Pearl Harbor did for the United States and Japanese relations in 1941.

Hockey Pictorial was only a few years old at the time my article appeared. Published in Montreal, it had only one New York outlet, the concession stand at Madison Square Garden. Apparently someone spotted the piece and showed it to Watson. Shortly thereafter I received a phone call from Ken McKenzie.

"We've got troubles," he said. "Watson didn't like your piece in the January issue."

"Frankly, I didn't expect him to like it," I replied. "So what?"

"So they've refused to sell *Hockey Pictorial* at the Garden. I'm going to have a lot of wasted magazines on my hands."

Watson wasn't powerful enough by himself to have the magazine removed from the Garden. That required the complicity of a higher authority, namely Muzz Patrick, the general manager. In my wildest dreams I couldn't imagine the Rangers stooping so low, particularly since the article not only was reasonably perceptive and well written but also was kind to Watson in many respects. "That doesn't matter," said Herb Goren, in his role as Watson's press mouthpiece. "Phil is furious with the *other* things that were said. There's nothing I can do about it. The magazine is no longer in the Garden."

Two thoughts came to mind: First, don't knuckle under to Watson and Patrick under any circumstances. Second, get that suppressed issue of *Hockey Pictorial* into the readers' hands somehow or other.

I phoned McKenzie and told him I'd buy every one of the issues he had shipped to the Garden and sell them on my own. Now, *I* got lucky. Bert Lee, Jr., the son of a former Rangers play-by-play announcer, was doing a nightly sports show accenting controversy. He agreed to have me on the air to discuss the magazine affair. Watson also was invited but declined. Thanks to Lee, I exposed the Watson embargo on the air and sold a few hundred copies to listeners who wrote in. Then Marvin Resnick, a Rangers fan and friend, sold several dozen more in the Garden balcony.

A few hundred more remained, so I asked Jacques Shiff, president of the Rangers fan club, for the opportunity to speak at a club meeting and sell some of the magazines. Shiff, no doubt concerned about the Garden's reaction, balked at first but later agreed to have me appear as a fan club guest. I am not proud of my performance that night. Overcome by the conflict with Watson and Patrick—and by what I believed was Goren's failure to support me—I appealed to the baser instincts of the fans. "What they are doing to me," I declared, "is worse than what you would expect from the Communists." A dozen issues were sold. About 150 remain in my closet.

I lost about $200 because of the *Hockey Pictorial* ban, but it was worth it. Enough magazines *were* sold to give the piece considerable publicity, and it made me something of a hero to newsmen on both sides of the border. (I recall Bob Hesketh of the Toronto *Telegram* followed up with a potent one-two verbal uppercut against Watson.) Soon word

49

filtered down from the Garden that the Rangers hierarchy was worried about me, especially since I showed no signs of easing the pressure on Watson.

The Rangers finished a distant fourth that season, fourteen big points behind third-place Boston. Montreal then wiped out Watson's club in five playoff games, thereby assuring Phil of a perfectly miserable off-season. About a month after the playoffs ended I received a phone call from Goren. "Why don't you come up to the Garden?" Herbie said with a half-whine that suggested that he was making an important request.

"What for?" I asked.

"Watson and Muzz want to talk to you. I'll be there, too. Maybe we can straighten things out."

I reluctantly agreed. All signs indicated that Patrick, Watson and Goren would pressure me into taking a more sympathetic tone in my writing about the Rangers, and I wasn't sure whether I was strong enough to handle all three.

The meeting was held in Patrick's big, gray-walled office in the rear of the hockey department. Muzz sat behind his desk while Watson and Goren occupied chairs along the wall. I took a seat on the opposite side of the door. Patrick shook my hand when I walked in. Watson stared straight ahead and made no move whatsoever, so I ignored him. After some idle banter about summer activities we got down to business. Patrick and Goren both spoke about the harsh quality of my stories, first mentioning my earlier piece in *The Hockey News*. "I have a right to disagree," I insisted. "Management made mistakes this season."

"You *don't* have all that right," said Goren. "Let's face it: *The Hockey News* is a league-financed publication. Nobody else writes the kind of stuff you do."

I couldn't quarrel with that. At this point I was close to reconciliation. Goren and Patrick had softened me up good. I was back in the very office where I had worked so heartily only two years ago for two men I had loved very dearly during that period. They had me by the nostalgia, if nothing else.

But Watson loused things up completely. Instead of minding his business and letting Goren and Patrick melt me, Phil sputtered, "Now, look, if you write one more bad story, you're through!"

I said nothing. Patrick said nothing. Finally, Goren suggested that we all shake hands and have a pleasant summer. We shook, but I still was smarting over Watson's ultimatum and left the Garden determined to ignore the coach's edict.

One of the unfortunate corollaries of going to war with Watson and Patrick was the negative effect on players I had befriended. It had become clear that any friend of Fischler's automatically had become an enemy of Watson's. Exhibit A was Aldo Guidolin.

Guidolin had become a good friend of mine during the disastrous 1954-55 season, mostly because he was an unpretentious athlete with a remarkable sense of humor and a birthplace—Forks of Credit, Ontario—that no other professional athlete could claim. The Rangers never could make up their minds whether to play Aldo on defense or as a forward. He played both positions equally well. Watson's solution was to use Guidolin as a penalty-killer, thoroughly wasting his talent. In time, Aldo was sent off to Providence where he became one of the best defensemen in the American League. I frequently wondered if it was worthwhile to write laudatory articles about Guidolin. Watson and Patrick went out of their way to disparage his abilities, and eventually my pro-Guidolin prose and their reaction became a house gag with other writers.

Any hope Guidolin had of rejoining the Rangers may have been dashed one night in Boston when Aldo tried to do me a favor. It was one of those old Saturday-Sunday weekend doubleheaders at Boston Garden, and the Rangers fan club was having its traditional excursion. I very much wanted to cover the games, but since the *Journal-American* had Dave Anderson on the hockey beat and I was merely covering for *The Hockey News*, I was ineligible to accompany the Rangers on their private train. Instead, I bought a round-trip coach ticket from the fan club and spent the weekend as a fan instead of a newspaperman.

By coincidence Guidolin had been recalled from Providence for the series because the Rangers lineup had been decimated by injuries. This appeared to be his last chance to persuade Watson and Patrick that he belonged, and I, for one, was praying hard for his success.

As luck would have it the Bruins bombed the Rangers on both nights. Watson, who hated losing to Boston more than any other team, was so livid you could have fried an egg on his forehead. It was sad all around, especially for fan club members, who now had to face the prospect of a milk-run coach ride home to New York.

Having made the trip several times in the past, I was among the least enthused members of the troupe as we crossed the marble waiting room of Boston's South Station. Just then, I felt a tap on my shoulder. I turned around and there was my pal, Aldo. "Where ya goin', buddy?" he asked.

"On the coach with the fan club," I told him.

Guidolin looked at me as if I had told him I was walking all the way to Manhattan. "Don't be silly," he said. "C'mon the Pullman with the team." I appreciated the gesture and sincerely hoped that Aldo would drop the subject then and there. But he now had made it a crusade to get me on the Rangers sleeper, and nothing I could say or do would persuade him otherwise, although I did marshall some good arguments.

"Now, look, Aldo," I concluded with finality, "I would

love to ride on the Pullman, but what would happen if Watson ever found out? You know how it is with me and Watson."

With a wave of the hand, Guidolin dismissed the suggestion and firmly grabbed my arm, leading me away from the fan club train. "Don't worry about Watson. We'll put you in an upper berth, close the curtains and he'll never know you're aboard. The way he's feelin' now, chances are he won't even come on the train."

We had walked out of the waiting room and on to the outdoor platform. A stiff wind cut across the tracks from the Charles River and sliced right through my overcoat. I was scared. The fan club train was about to leave, and I was irrevocably committed to the Rangers Pullman. But what if Watson suddenly came along and saw me boarding the train with Guidolin?

Aldo appeared so carefree about his caper that I began to suspect that I was being a nervous Nellie for no reason. The Pullman was hissing in the crisp Boston air as we boarded the steep steps. Aldo led the way into the narrow corridor flanked on both sides by curtains. Every so often one of the players—Andy Hebenton, Bill Gadsby, Andy Bathgate—walked by and more or less took for granted that I belonged on the train.

"Now what do I do?" I asked Guidolin when we arrived at his lower berth.

"Just taaake it eaassy," he replied in what best can be described as an Ontario drawl. "As soon as the train starts we'll put you in an empty upper. There must be at least a dozen of 'em in this car. In the meantime you stay here in my lower. We'll keep the curtains closed just in case Watson comes along."

Watson. I had just begun to forget him. The mere mention of his name sent a shudder up and down my legs. But Watson could never know I was on the train as long as the curtain was closed. There was only one problem. Aldo refused to keep the curtain closed. It was stifling in the lower berth so Guidolin opened the curtain about a quarter of the way. By cramming myself into a corner I was able to remain in the shadows out of full view of the aisle.

Suddenly, the train lurched, the couplings clanged and the stanchions of South Station began moving backward. We were off! There was no way now that Watson could get me off the train. Gump Worsley, the rotund goalie, walked by, saw Aldo and stopped for a chat. Gump's eyes cut sharply to the left. "What's *he* doing in there?"

"Shhh," said Aldo, "Watson's liable to find out, then I'll have hell to pay."

"Fuckin' right," Worsley said and walked away.

The lights of Boston were behind us as the Pullman bounced over the switches outside South station and plunged into the darkness for New York. The lights remained on in the team sleeper, however, and more of the Rangers stopped for a chat. They realized, of course, that I had become the Rangers' first stowaway. Everybody seemed to accept the fact that the joke was on Watson, and that made it all the more palatable.

I was beginning to enjoy it myself when Watson entered the car. Apparently he wanted only to pass through the club's sleeper enroute to his own bunk. Just why he turned as he reached Aldo's berth I'll never understand, but he did, and his eyes immediately caught me since I had just moved toward the center of the bed so that the overhead bulb focused on my face. The sight of me, the thoroughly unauthorized Fischler, sitting in a bunk reserved for Watson's team temporarily immobilized the coach.

I was prepared for two events, one following immediately after the other. Watson would denounce me in two languages for approximately forty-five seconds; then reach in and hurl me onto the floor. Since I was illegally aboard the train, I would not resist; nor would I object when he attempted to either throw me off the speeding express or turn me over to the railway police when we arrived in Providence, Rhode Island.

Instead Watson sputtered like a badly opened bottle of soda pop. When the words finally did come, they failed to gush out but fell slowly, almost sadly, out of his lips.

"What are you doing here?" he said.

I did not quite know how to put my predicament since I had no intention of mentioning that I was Guidolin's guest. There was only one thing to say: "I am sitting here." The simplicity of the explanation, not to mention its obvious truth, left Watson speechless. He riveted his eyes on mine for another moment, then turned and walked away never to be seen again that night.

Aldo fixed me an upper berth and I spent a rather uncomfortable night wondering what repercussions my escapade would have on me and my friend the utility player.

When I arrived at the *Journal American* office the next day, I received a phone call from Goren. He mildly reprimanded me and suggested that I get in touch with Patrick and apologize. He maintained a serious tone throughout, but I suspected that, deep down, Herbie appreciated my stowaway stunt. Patrick was surprisingly reasonable. I never discussed the matter with Watson.

A day later Guidolin was again demoted to the Rangers farm team in Providence. He never returned to the majors, but spent the next ten years mostly as Rangers property, in various farm teams. We will never know for sure, but Aldo and I have concluded after talking of this over the years that the Pullman episode formally ended his career with the Rangers (as well as my free rides).

As for Watson, he recovered from the 1956-57 debacle and led the Rangers to second place in 1957-58. But, as I had predicted in the *Hockey Pictorial* article, Watson would have to master his runaway emotions if he was going to succeed as an NHL coach. He didn't. In a collapse similar to the Brooklyn Dodgers' September fold of 1951, Watson's Rangers frittered away a nine-point lead over the Toronto Maple Leafs in March 1959 and finished out of the playoffs. Watson had lost control of the team and never could recapture his players' confidence. On November 12, 1959, I had the satisfaction of filing a story that I had wanted to write for more than two years. "WATSON DROPPED AS RANGERS COACH!"

IV

AT WAR WITH THE RANGERS—ROUND TWO, FISCHLER vs. PATRICK

In April 1964, while bedridden with hepatitis, I received a phone call from Max Kase, the *Journal-American's* sports editor. In my ten years as sports columnist for the Brooklyn section, I hadn't worked directly with Kase, although he had hired me. "When are ya gonna get well?" Kase demanded in that threatening gravel voice of his. "I wanna move ya into my department."

I told Max that the doctor had prescribed a long rest and that it would be August before I could start working again. "Okay," he said, his reply coated with unhappiness, "I'll just have to wait. Anyhow, I'm gonna move you onto the hockey beat, full time. So, getchaself in good shape."

Kase and I had always regarded each other with a sort of pleasant wariness. He knew I was obsessed with hockey and had been covering the Rangers for more than a decade in *The Hockey News,* but he feared that I wouldn't be interested in baseball, football and basketball assignments.

My own wariness arose from the knowledge that he was right. I enjoyed covering politics, the theater and general features for the *Journal-American* while doing my hockey-writing on the side. I was in no way interested in basketball, baseball and all of the other (what I considered nonconsequential) sports. But Kase was giving me a chance to climb up to the big time and, hopefully, become a hockey-writing superstar.

On August 1, I sat in front of a sports department typewriter and began writing my first story as the *Journal's* "hockey man." I replaced Dave Anderson, which was something like succeeding Gordie Howe. Although he didn't always get the choice assignments, Anderson was regarded by sportswriters as one of the top three jock journalists in the business and easily the best on the hockey beat.

Anderson's reputation never worried me, however. Deep down I knew that there was one basic—and vi-tal—difference between Dave and me. He liked hockey and enjoyed covering it, but he also enjoyed boxing, tennis, baseball and football. By contrast, I was passionately in love with and obsessed by hockey, and that enabled me to match Anderson in terms of the quality and quantity of hockey-writing.

Having been on the beat for ten years, I had long ago eschewed the ga-ga approach to the game. At first I became pleasantly disputatious about matters—or players—that irked me, but I soon moved to a more vigorous and antagonistic position. If I felt that someone deserved criticism or a team rated a rap, I didn't hesitate to deliver it; nor did I fail to realize that there would be repercussions.

My rambunctious style came to the fore when I wrote for McKenzie's *Hockey News*. Though the publication was never actually distributed under NHL auspices, McKenzie frankly admitted that the NHL supported his enterprise and made it quite clear that he did not want to offend any of the league governors.

Considering how my style had changed from saccharine to salty—the Phil Watson episode was a case in point—it was inevitable that I would collide and collide hard with the NHL Establishment. The trouble started when Bill Jen-nings, a tall, gray-haired attorney, moved in as the new power behind the Rangers early in the Sixties. A novice to hockey, Jennings nevertheless became enamoured of the sport and his team. He began reading *The Hockey News* and, in time, became more and more disenchanted with my occasionally hostile barbs.

Naturally, the criticism was deserved. Under the baton of Muzz Patrick, the Rangers had missed the playoffs five out of the six seasons from 1959 through 1964. Based on my interviews with players, coaches and managers, not to mention my own observations, I regarded Patrick as the chief culprit and wrote so. Automatically, my relationship with him deteriorated to the point where, in October 1964, it was virtually irreparable.

Patrick's coach was George "Red" Sullivan, a former Rangers, Black Hawks and Bruins center of modest abilities but a man with enormous zeal who had a knack for arousing the fans. I had always taken a dim view of Sullivan's antics, particularly because he pretended to be a fearless fighter but, to me, seemed more interested in creating a scene rather than engaging in it once the fuss actually had percolated.

As a coach, I considered him a total loss and blamed Patrick for the choice. Sullivan seemed somewhat shallow in his knowledge of the science of hockey and incapable of obtaining the most out of the Rangers' potential. Perhaps worst of all, he apparently did not get along with his ace goalie, Jacques Plante, with whom he had feuded when Plante played for the Canadiens and Sullivan with the Rangers.

This was tragic because Plante was one of the few super-stars on the Rangers—and was a stand-out in the NHL right through 1973. In New York, however, he was being wasted by Sullivan, who eventually encouraged his demotion to Baltimore in the minors.

The Rangers opened the 1964-65 season on October 13 at Madison Square Garden against the Montreal Canadiens. The visitors defeated New York, 3-0. At game's end, I headed for the dressing room, obtained my information and climbed back to the press box to write my story. Once again the Rangers seemed hell-bent for oblivion (they were to finish a poor fifth in the six-team league), and once again Patrick's grand plan appeared riddled with doubt.

My main story was directed at the game, however. When I finished, I wrote what we called a "sidebar," nothing more than a collection of short sentences, punctuated by three dots. Buried somewhere near the end of the sidebar was a mention about the crowd reaction. I wrote that some of the spectators had registered their protest against Patrick with a chant that had been heard in previous seasons—"Muzz must go!" That was the end of the item, but not the incident.

The next day, October 14th, was my day off, but I already had made it a practice to stay in contact with the Rangers' publicity office to be sure that I didn't miss any breaking news. I phoned John Halligan, who had succeeded Herb Goren as Rangers publicist, and asked him if anything was new. A young, genial fellow, Halligan betrayed a harsh strain in his voice that immediately told me trouble was ahead.

"I have bad news for you," he said. "As of the next game, you're not permitted into the Rangers' dressing room or the post-game conference room."

After gulping three times, I asked the logical question—why?

"Muzz didn't like what you wrote. Where did you get that stuff about the fans chanting, 'Muzz must go!'? That was just a crock, and you know it."

My original fear gave way to unmitigated anger. Not only did *I* hear the chants, I knew others had heard them and I knew people who were *doing* the chanting. Trying to remain as calm as possible, I told Halligan so, but he was unimpressed. "Do you realize what this act means in terms of freedom of the press?" I asked rather naively before fully understanding that Halligan merely was the lieutenant, carrying out his orders.

"There's nothing more for me to say," he said. "Good-bye."

The "good-bye" stuck in my craw for a long time. As I interpreted the scene, it was "good-bye" Ranger beat, good-bye job. Here I had covered one lousy game and I was thrown out of the box. I simply couldn't imagine Kase, who never had been overly enthused about hockey, thinking anything but the worst about me. I had automatically created a major problem for him since there was no way I could cover the games for an afternoon paper without visiting the dressing room and post-game conference room.

I couldn't reach Kase on Thursday and finally phoned him on Friday morning with news of the anti-Fischler boycott. He was livid—but at Patrick and the Garden, not me. "Those sons of bitches have a helluva nerve, he said. "You just sit tight and I'll get back to you."

That afternoon I had lunch with Joe Giaimo, an old roller hockey teammate, at Sloppy Louie's Restaurant near the Fulton Fish Market. Joe was a happy, rollicking sort and he cheered me up as much as possible under the circumstances—which wasn't much. I questioned my behavior under the game conditions. Did I do wrong in writing the note about "Muzz must go?" I had heard the chant, therefore I was correct in putting an item in the notes. But wouldn't it have been better just to omit the note and leave well enough alone? Well, it would have made that Friday lunch a lot more palatable, but it certainly would have contaminated my writing style.

After lunch, I returned to the newspaper. Kase called me over. "The ban has been lifted," he said with a straight face, leaning back in his swivel chair. "You're okay for the next game, Sunday night. And you're still my hockey man." Max explained that he had gone to the top and told Irving

Mitchell Felt, head man at the Garden, about the anti-Fischler movement. A wave of Felt's hand was enough to send anyone in the building into a dance. When Kase complained, Felt waved and Patrick lifted the gates for me.

I had won the battle, but the war with Patrick had just begun. Muzz was as prideful as I, and there were no signs of a truce after Kase had intervened on my behalf. Worse, tangential events blew up our feud even further. My dislike for Patrick had grown during the war with Watson, especially since Muzz appeared to condone much of Watson's anti-Fischler behavior. And, of course, the split between us deepened as I became more critical of Muzz in *The Hockey News.*

That, however, was small potatoes compared with the next step in the escalation, which followed right on the heels of the attempted dressing room ban. Unknown to most people on the hockey beat, I had been asked to edit a hockey annual for the 1964-65 season. The publisher was Haskell Cohen, then publicity director of the National Basketball Association and a man known for his multiplicity of projects. Two years earlier Cohen had sensed the hockey boom and asked me to do an annual for him. The first one I produced was relatively bland, and I vowed that the second, to appear in the fall of 1964, would be dynamite. It was.

One of the more potent articles was written by Al Robbins, then a top-flight *Journal-American* reporter and one of my closest friends in the newspaper business. Robbins' feature was about the Patrick brothers, Muzz and Lynn, and how they had failed to live up to their father's (Lester's) reputation as hockey administrators. The article was titled "No Longer Proud," and its first two paragraphs told it all:

"The name Patrick," wrote Robbins, "was once among the most honored in professional hockey. But no longer. Patrick today is synonymous with 'humpty-dumpty' hockey teams that are a discredit to the cities they represent and an insult to the fans who remain stubbornly loyal in the face of continuing adversity.

"For a decade now, Lynn and Muzz Patrick, the sons of Lester Patrick, the revered Silver Fox of yesteryear, have guided—misguided is perhaps the better word—the fortunes of the Boston Bruins and the New York Rangers. Except for occasional flashes of sparkle, both clubs have rolled over and played dead for the other four National Hockey League teams."

Robbins then unfolded a list of incidents and cases to make his point, quoting such respected hockey writers as Red Fisher of the Montreal *Star* ("The Rangers emerge as the biggest disappointment in some time.") And Tim Horgan of the Boston *Herald-Traveler* ("The Bruins have gone from bad to worse to a sorry, ludicrous mess.")

I'm sure that when Haskell Cohen commissioned me to assemble the annual, he had expected another one of the traditionally bland pieces of crap that abound in pulp sports publications. Certainly, he didn't expect anything as controversial as the Patrick piece.

The magazine was not scheduled to hit the stands until late October 1964, but bound copies already had made their way to the warehouse long before then. It seemed impossible at the time, but somehow Muzz Patrick learned about the Robbins article and raised holy hell with Cohen. When Haskell phoned me to tell me about the trouble, I began my worrying cycle all over again. Cohen was tight with Max Kase and in no position to antagonize Madison Square Garden, Patrick's employer. The seeds of some awfully dirty warfare were being spread, and I, for one, was less than optimistic.

"Patrick is threatening to sue me for libel," said Cohen. "Not only that, but he wants the magazine confiscated before it gets to the newsstands. I didn't tell him, but it's too late. They're already on their way."

"Don't you think he's bluffing you?" I asked.

"Maybe," replied Cohen, "but I'll have to talk it over with my lawyer."

According to Cohen, Patrick's case was based on two phrases used in the article. One was "humpty-dumpty hockey teams," used in the lead paragraph, and the other was the subhead of the title page: "Once The Most Honored Name In Hockey, Patrick Has Come To Be Synonymous With Policies Which Produce Punk Teams." Apparently, the expression "Punk Teams" stung as much as "humpty-dumpty."

Within a week, the magazine was on the newsstands and we sat tight to see what would develop, if anything. Day after day, I waited for a call from Cohen, but nothing more happened. In the meantime, I continued to plug away at my job with the *Journal.* From October 13th, the night of the home opener at the Garden, through October 25th, when Chicago embarrassed the Rangers, 5-2, in New York, Patrick's club had not won a game. Perhaps it was the personnel, perhaps it was the coach. Certainly, Red Sullivan appeared weak to me, especially since Marcel Paille was playing goal while the great Plante was vegetating in Baltimore.

I had not forgotten Plante—we had dinner together at McCarthy's Steak House on his first night in New York after the Rangers had signed him in the summer of 1963—and was astonished at a wire service story that was buried in the back of the *Herald-Tribune.* The dateline was Baltimore and the subject was Plante. In several well-chosen words, Jacques the ripper tore the Rangers organization to shreds, criticizing everything from management to coaching. It was a devastating story, yet it appeared nowhere else and even was hidden in the *Tribune.*

I felt this was a major piece and had to be kept alive. There was only one thing for me to do: contact Plante directly in Baltimore and get him to corroborate what I had read in the *Trib.* In the meantime, I checked around to learn whether Plante's attitude toward the Rangers was, as suggested, so terribly down. All my sources in Baltimore confirmed that point, and then I reached Plante himself.

I probed tenderly, but he was more direct than I expected. "The dressing room, for one thing," Plante said, "is a shit house." And he went on from there to set off verbal bombs under the Patrick regime. On Wednesday, October 28th, 1964, the story made a headline in the *Journal-American*. That night the Rangers were host to the Bruins. I suspected that some sort of retribution would be in order from Patrick, but I wasn't quite sure which route he would ply for the counterattack. He could, of course, have ignored the story. This might have been the best course, except that his bosses, Irving Mitchell Felt and Bill Jennings, must have read the article and surely were stung as hard as Patrick. Another possibility was simply to issue a disclaimer at the post-game press conference and parry any questions that might arise at that time. A few moments before the opening face-off, I finally got the first clue about Patrick's strategy.

Halligan, the club press agent, walked up and down the press area distributing invitations to a special press conference scheduled for the following day. The announcement was suitably vague about the subject, but within minutes word leaked out that it concerned the Plante story. That's as far as accuracy went. From there an assortment of rumors spread in different directions, each of which I found worrisome. My mind whirled over the things Muzz might say, and on top of that I was concerned that he just might do something about the threatened suit against Haskell Cohen's annual.

Ironically, the Rangers looked good that night, defeating Boston 3-1. I did the usual dressing room-conference room routine, wrote my story and then headed home, debating with myself over what I should do. The easiest course, at least superficially, was simply to ignore the Thursday press conference. Having covered the Wednesday night game, I had Thursday off and therefore had every reason not to attend the Garden meeting. But I was curious, and, though I feared the ominous consequences, there was a sense of urgency in the air that suggested I should be there, no matter what happened. Armed with two rolls of English lemon drops, I took the subway to the Garden, arriving fifteen minutes before the scheduled conference.

The Rangers' office in the old Madison Square Garden was located on the third floor. Upon leaving the elevator and entering the office, newsmen traditionally turned right and headed straight for the publicity office. From there, one could then move on to visit the general manager or coach, if invited.

I took the traditional turn right, desperately trying to conceal any signs of nervousness. My arms were loaded with papers. I made certain to gather all my notes on the Plante conversations (which I had carefully saved) as well as the wire story out of Baltimore that had appeared in the *Herald-Tribune* and any other written material that would support my case, if such support became necessary.

Halligan's office already was filling with newsmen, most of whom were my friends. Leonard Lewin of the *Post* had arrived along with Benny Olan of The Associated Press and we chatted offhandedly. Dick Sorkin, a young *Newsday* reporter, was also there as was a chap from UPI.

Word came that the press conference was about to begin. We all filed out of the publicity room and walked down the hall, past the framed photos of old-time Rangers and Willard Mullin cartoons. This was the same office in which I virtually lived—and died—with the Rangers during 1954-55, and now, I felt, they were going to try and kill me.

We walked through the cubby-hole office of Pat Doyle, the team's traveling secretary, turned right into Muzz Patrick's huge room overlooking 49th Street and the Belvedere Hotel. Patrick, awesomely large, sat behind the big, brown desk while Bill Jennings, the Rangers president, puffed on a cigarette at his side. There were a few seats for the reporters but the crowd was so large that many newspapermen, including myself, stood against the wall facing Patrick. Then off to the right, I suddenly spied Jacques Plante. I was damned scared and nervously unwrapped a lemon drop in my pocket and quickly popped it into my mouth as Patrick began talking.

He alluded to my story about Plante and the Rangers that had appeared in Wednesday's *Journal-American*. Muzz said Plante had been asked to come up from Baltimore to comment on the article. He then beckoned to Plante who immediately began a lengthy denial of just about everything I had written.

Up until this point I had not decided on any particular strategy, mostly because I had no idea what was going to happen. But as Plante unraveled his tale of being misquoted, my overwhelming sense of fear once again turned to raw anger. "That lying bastard," I said to myself. "I can't let him go on without protest."

The veteran goalie seemed to have captured the audience of reporters like a President giving an inaugural address. From the contented look on his face, it seemed as if the last thing in the world he expected was an interruption, let alone a denial. I broke in. My words were neither shrill nor especially muffled. "I disagree with what you say," I blurted. "What's more I have my notes here and will read what you told me...."

If Plante was surprised, Patrick, who seemed a trifle under the weather, was flabbergasted. As I began to fidget for my proper notes page, he boomed: "Shut up, you prick!"

The words penetrated and hurt, but they only served to reinforce my feeling that my side had to be heard—and had to be heard in front of Plante, Patrick, Jennings and anybody else who wanted to make an accusation.

After Patrick's outburst had subsided, Plante continued. Again he tried to contradict my story. This time, I whipped

67

out the *Herald-Tribune* wire story, which seemed to surprise Plante and Patrick as much as it had me when I read it days before. "Judging by what you say," I stated, "there seems to be a difference between what you say and this article."

Patrick shouted again. For the second time in five minutes I was called a prick. For me it was some sort of record. Patrick's second burst of invective appeared to stun the audience more than the first. It was loud and hard and the target was unmistakeable. Subjective as I was, I could swear that it made the usually implacable Jennings wince.

In a matter of minutes the press conference was over. I could have headed straight for the stairway, just outside Patrick's office, with a few other reporters but I didn't want it to seem as if I was running. Instead, I walked back to Halligan's room with Sorkin and one or two other fellows. I tried to force myself into a calm pose, but it hardly was possible. Sorkin later wrote that I looked white and made some other gratuitous remark about my lack of calm. I later discussed it with him and got absolutely no consolation. I was surprised since I had thought until then that Sorkin was firmly in my corner.

After about ten minutes of nervous chatter, I finally left Halligan's office satisfied that I had not been chased. Once I reached 49th Street, I fully realized how thoroughly shaken I was. My hands were trembling and my heart sounded like the bass drum in a marching band. I frankly didn't know what I was going to do next.

I was afraid that Plante and Patrick had convinced the reporters that I was full of shit and that poor Jacques had been victimized. I needed some advice in a hurry so I phoned Stan Saplin, who had been so much help in the past. He told me to meet him for dinner at the New York University Club near Times Square and we would work out a battle plan.

Saplin was marvelous. First he calmed me. Then, he

assured me that I had done no wrong. Finally, he suggested that I go back to the *Journal* and write a story about the episode, keeping it as light-hearted as possible. By the time he got through with me I was so anxious to write my story, I felt like flying straight over the rooftops to the *Journal* building.

The article itself was a gem. It was light but with enough harpoons to get my point across. Patrick snapped his fingers and Jacques was nimble, Jacques was quick, Jacques jumped over the hockey stick. The night sports editor liked it enough to put it right up on page one of the section, although it was an off day for hockey news. I felt splendid.

Only one thing was missing—support from my colleagues. Since I had not been home all day, there was no way I could know how many writers had called, but the next day I picked up the *Post* and there was a full column by Lenny Lewin, blasting Patrick and supporting my stand. I breathed easily again, although the prospect of facing a full season with Muzz was deadly.

I left the office that Friday evening somewhat numb over the events of the past few days. I needed some relief, some relaxation. I looked forward to Saturday when our family would all get together to celebrate my cousin Paul's Bar Mitzvah at a synagogue in Long Island. It was late morning when I arrived at the temple. There were the usual familial embraces, jokes and greetings. I finally made my way to cousin Paul, a marvelous lad with a splendid wit. Even then, he was regarded as one of the funnier people in a funny family.

I shook his hand. "Congratulations," *he* said to me.

"*You* are congratulating me on your Bar Mitzvah. What for?"

Paul turned on his wry smile. "Don't tell me you don't know that Muzz Patrick was just fired."

The words didn't quite filter through. "Yeah," he

repeated, realizing that I was uncertain. "Muzz Patrick *was* fired. It was on the radio this morning. And I'm not kidding either."

By now I was pretty sure that he wasn't kidding, but not certain. I bolted from the crowd and headed for the nearest phone. My fingers hardly could dial fast enough as I tried to reach Lew King, the assistant sports editor of the *Journal,* who was running the desk that morning. My moment of jubilation was immediately dulled. "Where the fuck are you?" King demanded. "We been tryin' to locate you all mornin'. Patrick got the axe and we wanted you to write the story."

I told King I would be back in the office as quickly as possible. When I finally made it back to the *Journal,* King explained that the Garden did what it could to keep the story from hitting with any kind of impact. "Don't feel bad," he said. "They sent the release around by messenger late last night and didn't even deliver it to us. It took a while til we found the damn thing laying on some desk. I guess they thought we'd never find it and never write anything."

Typically, the release ducked the point. Patrick was to be promoted to a higher position in the Garden executive monolith. He would be replaced by Emile "The Cat" Francis, who had been the club's assistant general manager and was a man whom I respected and trusted as a friend.

I phoned Francis and congratulated him on the promotion, one for which I felt somewhat responsible. He thanked me and suggested I come in and visit with him privately early the next week. I accepted. Two days later Francis sat back in his chair, puffed on a Lucky Strike and calmly asked me just how the trouble with Patrick had begun. I spun out my tale of woe, and when I finished we shook hands. "You can be sure this won't happen to you as long as I'm general manager of the Rangers," Francis said, pumping my hand again.

He was wrong.

V

I TEACH
ED GIACOMIN
HOW TO PLAY GOAL

The ambition of every newspaperman is to "scoop" the opposition and come up with a hot story before the rival papers get wind of it. My first major scoop developed in May 1965 and happened in a very curious way. I had become a matchmaker for a Buffalo newspaperman named Charlie Barton, and in return for every girl's telephone number I gave him, Charlie rewarded me with a scoop.

Barton, who died in 1972, worked for the Buffalo *Courier-Express* when Buffalo still played in the American Hockey League, the number one farm league (including Cleveland, Springfield, Providence, Hershey, etc.) that sent talent on to the National Hockey League. A lovable bachelor, Barton had the best contacts of any newspaperman I have ever met on the hockey beat. He was a Canadian, lived in St. Catherines, Ontario—a short drive from Buffalo and Toronto—and seemed to have had dealings with just about every player, coach, manager or owner who ever came down the pike.

Barton was especially close to Reuben Pastor, the Pepsi-Cola distributor who owned the Buffalo AHL franchise.

Pastor was able to get just about every bit of inside information that seeped out of the AHL as well as the NHL. Since Charlie and Ruby were "lantzmen," as they say in Yiddish, Ruby told Charlie everything that happened behind the scenes.

In 99 per cent of the cases, the information was off the record and Barton couldn't use it in his own paper. But as far as Charlie was concerned that didn't mean I couldn't use it, provided that I "protected" my source. On all of Charlie's leads there were at least a dozen possible sources, so he was pretty well-protected when the story made print.

I first met Barton one day when he stopped over at the Rangers' publicity office. Herb Goren was still the team's p.r. man, and he took a paternal interest in Charlie—something like a Jewish father who wanted to see his middle-aged son get married, already! Herbie suggested that I fix up Charlie with a nice Jewish girl. I phoned a very pleasant and attractively buxom girl I knew and she agreed to go out with Charlie. I got myself a date and the four of us had dinner at the Overseas Press Club in Manhattan. It was obvious that Charlie was infatuated with Ellie and equally obvious that he now regarded me as a very dear friend. Later, their romance fizzled—she wouldn't move to St. Catherines and he wouldn't move to Brooklyn—after almost reaching the engagement stage. But Charlie and I had become close friends and periodically he'd visit New York in search of a wife, and I would, theoretically, try to find him one.

In the interim we would be on the phone once or twice a week, exchanging delectable tidbits about the hockey world. He called one day early in May 1965. "I've got a real hot one for you," he said. Then, after a pause, came Charlie's traditional words of caution: "But, remember, you didn't get it from me!"

The story was something less than a blockbuster but a

good one nonetheless. The Rangers had traded four play-ers—Marcel Paille, Aldo Guidolin, Sandy McGregor and Jim Mikol—to Providence (formerly a Rangers farm team and now privately owned) for Ed Giacomin, a goaltender who had never played a single game in the majors.

At the time, the Rangers goalie was Jacques Plante. As mentioned earlier he had been nothing but trouble for the front office, although his flair did bring people into the Garden. At twenty-six years of age, Giacomin was to be groomed as Plante's eventual replacement, perhaps in three or four years.

It was a meaningful story to me because I wanted to show Emile Francis and Bill Jennings that I could beat them on their own announcements. And I did.

Thanks to Barton, the *Journal-American* broke the Giacomin story before the Rangers publicist could crank out his release. Jennings and Francis were suitably embarrass-ed, and I was riding high. Just to show it was no fluke, I scooped the Rangers again within a matter of weeks—this time with the announcement that Jack Gordon had been hired as assistant general manager. The faces on Francis and Jennings were never redder, thanks, of course, to Charlie Barton.

Jennings and I had been getting along better, however. In a weak moment he asked me to help him lure Vaclav Nedomansky, Czechoslovakia's best player, to New York. I had met Nedomansky during a visit to Bratislava and had written glowingly about his hockey ability. On my return, I received an invitation to confer with Jennings. He asked me how I could help him obtain Nedomansky. I referred him to friends of mine who then were working with the Czech tourist bureau. After several weeks of discussion, the plans—at one point there was talk of inspiring Nedomansky to defect—were shelved.

Giacomin made his first appearance in a Rangers uniform

at training camp in the autumn of 1965. Within four months he had emerged as the most important member of the team. That summer Plante unexpectedly retired, leaving the Rangers with a grand total of no experienced goaltenders with which to start the season.

"Believe me," said Charlie Barton, "Giacomin is not going to help your club. He's not a big-leaguer."

Having grown to respect Barton's opinion, I covered the Rangers training camp at Kingston, Ontario, looking for Giacomin's flaws. They were abundant. His style was virtually nonexistent. He could be beaten with high shots, low shots—in fact just about any shots that didn't precisely hit him in the belly. Charlie was right.

Fortunately for the Rangers, they had another goaltender in camp who outplayed Giacomin every time he stepped on the ice. His name was Cesare Maniago and he reminded me of a brontosaurus with his small head perched on top of a long, long body. When Maniago kicked out a puck, his spread-eagled move suggested the grace of a Radio City Music Hall Rockette. Cesare had something that Giacomin didn't have then—or now, for that matter—a classic style.

He also was good copy. Maniago liked to talk about goaltending, about his mother's spaghetti and about how Francis was screwing him out of the Rangers first-string goaltending job. "I think I belong with the big team," he said one evening while Tony Merenghi of the Newark *Star-Ledger* and I were standing under the hotel marquee, watching the raindrops fall.

"That's right," said Tony, "you do. And you will!"

I knew better. Insecure in his job and worried about Jennings' opinion of him, Francis needed more than anything to justify the Giacomin deal. It hardly mattered that Maniago was the best goalie in camp. When the 1965-66 season began, Giacomin was standing between the pipes. Maniago had been sent to the minors.

My relationship with Giacomin had been relatively good up until this point. That is, he would talk to me, although I sometimes wondered why I bothered interviewing him since his answers usually ranged from "that's hard to say" to "that's *really* hard to say." Like most players before the advent of six-figure salaries, he was a pleasant enough chap whose only fault was that he was not good enough to play in the National Hockey League—if you can call that a fault.

But he did and, wonder of wonders, he played surprisingly well in the first weeks of the season. More than anyone, I helped the Giacomin cause by first detecting his one exceptional trait—an ability to skate and stickhandle with the puck better than any other goalie, and a willingness to do so. He seemed to always be on the go. Hence, a six-column banner headline in the *Journal-American* established Giacomin's image: *"GOALIE A GO-GO."*

The nickname was good, or bad, enough to be adapted by the Rangers publicity office, and thus Giacomin became a name, if not a very good goaltender. As in major league baseball, the veterans in hockey usually need about a month to locate the weaknesses in rookies. Exactly one month after Giacomin's debut his weak underbelly as a goaltender began to show. The dashes away from his net that earned the "Goalie A Go-Go" tag now began to result in goals for the enemy. The Rangers began losing and Giacomin, because he deserved it, was fingered as the culprit.

I did not look forward to indicting Giacomin in the *Journal-American,* or *The Hockey News* for that matter, because I felt a special warmth for the man. After all, he *was* the subject of my first major scoop. He had been cooperative if not expecially eloquent when I interviewed him, and, away from the strains of the rink, he was a genuinely affable and occasionally humorous man. But he was a lousy goalie at the time, and I, for one, was not going to ignore this point in print. As the Giacomin negatives began appearing in my columns, the distance widened between the goalie and me. One afternoon I phoned him at home for information about a story I was writing. His wife Marg answered in a steely voice that nearly punctured my eardrum.

"No!" she said, adroitly concealing a shout, "Ed is not home."

"When will he be home?"

"I don't know."

"Will you have him call me when he gets home?"

"I'll give him the message."

The return call never came, so I phoned again, and Mrs. Giacomin advised me, sounding much harsher if that were possible, that she had no idea when Ed would return and didn't know whether he would be able—or willing—to phone me back. I got the message. And I no longer liked Ed Giacomin. But, like him or not, I had an obligation to continue interviewing him whenever possible if the story demanded it.

A day or two after the cold conversation with Mrs. Giacomin, I began suffering guilt pangs over her husband and his plight. It was Christmas 1965, and I felt I owed the embattled young goalie a gift of good cheer. I got a brainstorm. Maybe it would help Giacomin if I could explain in print just how difficult it was to stand in front of a four-foot high by six-foot wide goal cage and face shots coming at more than 100 miles per hour.

I decided the most vivid method of making the point was to put on the goal pads *myself* and have a member of the Rangers skate headlong at me in enough different ways to give me an idea of Giacomin's daily ordeal as a goalie. Since my contacts with Ranger coach Emile Francis and publicist John Halligan were then good and I agreed to sign a waiver saying I wouldn't sue the Rangers in case of injury, it was a simple matter to set up the stunt.

It was agreed to do it after the New Year on an afternoon when the Rangers would be practicing at Skateland, their workout rink in suburban New Hyde Park, Long Island. My closest friend on the Rangers at the time was Rod Gilbert, the high-scoring right wing. He agreed to be the shooter against me in the one-on-one operation.

Francis agreed to fit me out with the complete goaltender's garb except for the skates, which were my own. Masks were virtually unheard of in those days, despite their use by Jacques Plante, so naturally I was not going to wear one. Actually, I had hoped to wear Giacomin's equipment to better personalize the story. I assumed that once he realized what it was all about he would agree, but we never got around to that.

A day before the stunt was to be executed, the Rangers sent Giacomin to Baltimore and recalled Cesare Maniago.

I was both stunned and gratified by the announcement. Ever since that evening in Kingston, standing under the hotel marquee with Maniago and Tony Marenghi, I was convinced that Maniago deserved the first-string goaltender's job. The Rangers decision also confirmed my stories that Giacomin didn't belong in the NHL, and that made me feel good, too, although I remained somewhat depressed about the manner in which Giacomin was treated. But he was young and he would get another chance if he managed to learn anything while playing in Baltimore.

I decided to proceed with my foolhardy masquerade anyway. On Friday, January 7, 1966 I arrived at Skateland with my pair of CCM Tackaberry skates under my arm and a considerable weight in my head. "Why?" I kept asking myself, "am I doing this stupid thing?" I was afraid of getting hurt. Gilbert had been instructed to shoot the puck as he would in a game. And I was embarrassed about the ribbing I surely would take from the players, some of whom already had made it clear that they resented my criticism of Giacomin.

But my journalistic radar also was blipping away, informing me loud and clear that this would be one hell of a good story. Especially since George Plimpton already was making a bundle from *Paper Lion,* the book based on his tryout with the Detroit Lions football team.

My heart beat a little easier when I arrived in the dressing room. Thank Heaven Giacomin was gone, the players were on the ice and nobody was around but trainer Frank Paice and a photographer from the *Journal-American.* Paice, an old buddy from my publicist days with the Rangers, helped me with the equipment. "I'm giving you Maniago's pads and gloves," he said. "They may be a little big on you but what the hell."

Sure, what the hell! The last time I played goal was in December 1947. Our roller hockey team, the Woodside Whippets, was forced by a blizzard to temporarily cancel its schedule until the snow disappeared from the streets. We decided to take our skates and sticks and play ice hockey on frozen Central Park Lake. I played goal for five minutes wearing two old seat cushions for pads. I managed pretty well until Jim Hernon lifted a shot to my right. I had the puck lined up all the way and handled it perfectly. My right leg flashed out in the classic style of Bill Durnan, and I deflected the puck harmlessly to the side with the inside of my kneecap. Only one thing went wrong. The adhesive tape which bound the cushion to my leg had come loose and at the split-second when my leg lurched to make the save the tape came off, leaving me with nothing but bare knee confronting the cold, hard piece of rubber.

While my teammates cheered the save, captured the puck and skated in the other direction, I remained horizontal on the frozen park lake experiencing a brand of pain I had never felt before, or have since. It had the elements of an endless electric shock combined with the pricking of a hypodermic needle, all centered in the left side of my kneecap.

Suddenly, I looked up and was horrified to discover that the opposition had recaptured the puck and was skating headlong in my direction. "Fer Chrissake, get up!" my sympathetic defensemen shouted at me.

Desperately trying to inspire myself with thoughts of my heroic professional heroes, I summoned all the energy and courage at my command and tried to lift myself into position with my good left leg. I was upright for a brief moment just as the opposition launched another shot at me. Unfortunately, my right leg was somehow not there and I collapsed to the ice again with remarkable ease.

How clever of me! The attacker's shot was an ice-skimmer and smacked into my leg as I fell sideways. Once again I heard cheers. My teammates actually thought I had fallen to the ice on purpose to make the big save. I promptly smothered the puck and forced a face-off. Nobody would believe the pain I still felt in the leg, but somehow I had to get out of that torture chamber.

"Lemme go back up at forward," I suggested.

My colleagues were reluctant to part with so expert a goalie, but they also felt I should be rewarded for my efforts. As unobtrusively as possible, I fell to my side, rolled over in the snow and gained a respite by removing the cushions. I squeezed five minutes out of the operation by which time the pain had subsided. I returned to the forward position, vowing never to play goal again.

Now, twenty one years later I was going to be goaltender against Rod Gilbert, one of the best shots in hockey.

Trainer Paice had finished helping me put the pads on, so there was no hiding anymore in the dressing room. I picked up the fat goalie stick and galumphed along the rubber matting that leads to the rink feeling very much like Dumbo the Elephant. Once I reached the sideboards I decided that I had not made a wise move. "Fischler," shouted Ranger forward John McKenzie, "go back to the typewriter." Soon, there was a chorus of similar barbs, and I didn't handle them very well.

At last, Francis whistled an end to the workout. This was my cue. I skated onto the ice and immediately was pleased that I hadn't fallen on my face. After two turns around the rink I began to feel cocky. A few of the Rangers remained on the ice and began passing the puck to me. It was difficult to field passes with the bulky goalie's stick, but I handled myself better than I thought I would. It was fun. "Bring on Gilbert," I demanded.

Any suggestion of cockiness disappeared the moment I took my position in front of the nets. Suddenly, I felt as though I were standing in front of the Grand Canyon. I didn't want to let on that I couldn't cope with the situation, however, so I waved off Gilbert with a contemptuous swing of my stick and told him I had to prepare the crease for my goaltending. I remembered how every goalie I had ever seen skated back and forth in front of the net scraping up ice. "Perhaps," I observed, "I can scrape up enough to keep the puck out."

Gilbert was becoming impatient. We agreed that he would have fifteen breakaway attempts. Francis would be the judge. "No lifting," I whispered to Gilbert behind Francis' back. I remembered those street corner roller hockey games when lifting at a goalie's unprotected ankles was strictly verboten. So what if I had pads on now? Rod didn't go along. "Okay," I countered, "no spearing. Not even the league allows that." Reluctantly he agreed.

During my two hours waiting to go on the ice I had carefully observed Don Simmons, the Rangers' spare goalie, block shots during a scrimmage. "There's really nothing to it," I thought to myself, confirming a theory I had entertained for years in the press box. "Why, even a sportswriter can do that."

"You ready?" Gilbert shouted, and before I could say "not yet," he was churning up the ice, the puck bouncing around his stick like a jumping bean. I remember thinking that a puck blasted by Gilbert travels upwards of 110 miles an hour. But even when he's trying to deke (fake) and tuck it behind the goalie, the rubber would be hard to track with radar. So, here he came. I thought of the goaltender's adage, "you can't stop what you can't see" and I comforted myself with that. Rod slithered to the left. I slithered with him and dove for the puck. That was the last I saw of it.

Imagine my surprise when I looked up and discovered that Gilbert was on the right and the puck was in the net!

"I dare you to do that again," I said, feigning anger.

"I accept," said Gilbert, who then employed thirteen different methods to beat me. He is very deceitful that way. But he was lucky and I let Francis have a piece of my mind.

"How can you expect a goalie to stop shots if you let him rot on the bench for two hours in the cold?" I shouted. He laughed. There were lots of laughs but, so far, no saves.

Now we were down to the last shot, and I was pretty down on myself. I had missed fourteen out of fourteen. The Rangers undoubtedly would remove my name from their negotiation list. My reputation was growing so bad I feared I might even be demoted to the minors.

Gilbert cruised into view. The look in his eyes told me he would let go a high, hard one. Although I didn't see it, the whizzing sound indicated that the puck was flying to my left. I flung out my left arm, closed my eyes and hoped for the best. Then a miracle happened. My left glove flew off my hand, hit the puck in the air and knocked the puck to the side. I doubt that Ed Giacomin could make a save like that on his best day.

At last the "game" was over. Gilbert and I trundled to the

locker room. Despite my last-second heroics I was a broken man. I hoped the coach would lock the dressing room door.

I didn't want to talk to the press.

Gilbert undressed and left the dressing room in ten minutes, which was just about the time I needed to catch my breath. It was an interesting experience, and I was sure it would make a good story. Too bad Giacomin couldn't be around to read it.

I was so busy trying to open the leather straps and remove the goalie pads that I didn't notice a man enter the room and walk to the locker in the opposite corner. The thunk of one fifteen-pound goalie pad falling atop the other caused me to look up. A little shiver of remorse sent goose pimples along my bare arms and down my legs. It was Giacomin, there to pack his equipment for the trip to the minors.

I desperately wanted to apologize for *anything* I had written that had hurt him, and I wanted to shake his hand to at least suggest a feeling of amiability if not friendship. But nothing came out.

His eyes remained riveted to the equipment bag. The packing finished, he tossed the bag over his shoulder and started toward the door. I looked up. "Sorry about what happened, Ed," I blurted. "Sorry!"

He didn't look at me; he turned toward the door, his eyes staring straight ahead with the kind of optical penetration one uses when taking an eye test. He didn't say a word, didn't slam the door, just headed for the parking lot.

As it happened, he wasn't away from New York very long. He played seven games for Baltimore in the American League and then returned to the Rangers where he soon became a star and their number one goalie. At a hockey writers' dinner two years later, I presented Giacomin with a plaque which my colleagues among the writers had awarded him for his competence as Rangers goalie. This time he looked at me, said "Thank you" and shook my hand.

VI

A FEW PRECIOUS
DAYS WITH
ROCKET RICHARD

When I first began following hockey as a kid, "The Rocket" Richard was beginning to emerge as the game's most prolific goal-scorer. In 1945, the year of my Bar Mitzvah, Richard scored fifty goals *in fifty games,* a record that has never been matched.

Being a Toronto Maple Leafs fan, I naturally regarded Richardian feats with fear and awe, but my admiration for the man never ceased, and as I grew older and began writing about hockey, I zeroed in on the Rocket whenever I could.

At first I found him a rather distant person. His command of English still was shaky and he tended to shy away from non-French-speaking reporters. I got absolutely nowhere with him until April 20, 1958, when I drove to Boston with two friends, Joe Breu and Dave Perlmutter, to watch the sixth game of the Stanley Cup finals between the Bruins and Canadiens.

It was a remarkable event in my life for two reasons—I at last met and talked with Richard, and I barely survived getting punched in the mouth by an irate Boston fan. The near miss occurred midway in the game while I energetically cheered the Canadiens on to what was to be a 5-3 victory and the Stanley Cup.

As so often happens in fan-to-fan confrontations, a Bruins' follower sitting to my left took exception to my remarks about his team. I had just popped a peppermint Life Saver into my mouth before the decibel count began rising and the Boston chap and myself rose out of our seats. (Fortunately, we were separated by an iron pipe divider that split up sections of the arena.)

In any event he yelled something at me to the effect that I might go screw myself, and I began replying when the peppermint Life Saver catapulted, accidentally, out of my mouth and hit him square in the eye. Fortunately, my friend Joe Breu had been keeping an Argus eye on the proceedings and swiftly hurled himself between us as the peppermint Life Saver descended from the Boston fan's eye down to his lapel and finally the floor. It was one of Breu's better moves because while separating us he managed to push me into his seat while taking over my place next to the fan. A laconic type, Breu couldn't have cared less which team won and thereby provided an excellent buffer between us two hotheads.

Once the Canadiens had won the Cup, I changed from my role of fan into newspaperman. I had been working for *The Hockey News* at the time and had proper credentials for the Montreal dressing room, which was a tiny, steamy area that seemed too small for twenty players let alone the fifty plus newsmen and photographers who somehow jammed their way into the jubilant quarters.

Although the Rocket had enjoyed splendid years earlier in his career, he still was playing marvelously and looked like a proud lion as he stepped out of the shower and began toweling himself before the eager reporters. He was unusually hairy, an aspect that embellished his masculine image, and quite eloquent despite his earlier problems with the English language.

After most of the newsmen had finished their questioning, I approached the Rocket, pumped his large hand and talked briefly about his future (he was to retire two years later in 1960). Considering the circumstances, he was most pleasant and I thanked him profusely for his time. There still was more of the fan in me than the reporter, and the mere act of talking with Maurice Richard for a few minutes was the equivalent of a pilgrim spending an hour with the Pope.

I met the Rocket a few more times, and following his retirement I phoned him from time to time for his opinions on various stories. In 1965, when I was writing hockey for the *Journal-American,* the Rangers were on the lookout for a coach. Richard seemed like a natural to me, especially since he had never been given a chance to coach by the Canadiens. I called the Rocket and discussed the matter with him. He said he was interested, but I detected an air of melancholy in his voice. Even then, there were signs that he had become disenchanted with the manner in which the Establishment was warping the hockey world.

Nothing came of my proposal that Richard coach the Rangers. My own feeling was that his close family ties would have prevented him from leaving his native Montreal. I also was certain that Emile Francis, who had become general manager of the Rangers, was afraid that Richard's glow would completely overshadow him. It would have been too demoralizing an experience for the Francis ego.

I had almost no contact with the Rocket again until four years later, in the spring of 1969 when Fred Katz, the managing editor of *Sport* magazine, phoned and suggested that I co-author an article with Richard. It was to focus on hockey's overzealous expansion program which had already begun with the creation of six new teams which made a total of twelve in the NHL. (There are now 16 NHL teams, and the World Hockey Association, created in 1971, has twelve.) The absurd dilution of talent had deteriorated the game to the point where the quality of the NHL had dipped to minor league level.

The idea appealed to me but, the trick was to win Richard's support. A call to Montreal was all I needed. The Rocket agreed to meet me and my tape recorder at the Mount Royal Hotel for a long discussion on the abysmal state of major league hockey. I was rather excited about a reunion with Richard and wondered whether he had changed much since I last had seen him. He had.

He now spoke English with the fluency of a native Torontonian. He weighed about 220, nearly thirty pounds over his playing weight. Every so often he betrayed a double-chin, especially while smiling, which he often did.

If there was one major change in the Rocket's personality it was his new ability to relax. The tension that had been so obvious during his playing days had disappeared, and he leaned back, puffed on a big cigar and occasionally sipped a glass of Scotch. He told me that he was working on his "second family." His children born during his playing career had grown, and he had new little ones around the house. He seemed totally pleased with domestic life.

By contrast, he was thoroughly disenchanted with the big-league hockey scene. Each week he dictated a column called "Maurice Richard Speaks" for a French-Canadian paper. Once I had seen the column, I realized that the Rocket and I would have no trouble at all. Our feelings about the game were virtually identical, and what he felt about hockey 1969, compared with hockey 1959 and hockey 1949, reflected exactly how I felt about The Game.

"The game of hockey," said Richard, "is simply not the game it was in my day. Shooting was more accurate then. Passing was cleverer. Stickhandling was an art practiced not by just a few but by many. And, most important, there was much more individuality. In short, the game is hurting today, and if you want to find the causes, you have to start with the biggest one: expansion."

The Rocket obviously was burned because his achievement of scoring fifty goals in a season was becoming more and more meaningless as goals became cheaper and cheaper to obtain. "There was a time," said Richard, "when it was an honor to score twenty goals in a season. It was like hitting .300 in baseball. But now twenty goals don't mean beans.

"You know what else had changed?" he continued. "The game isn't as tough as it used to be. You can count on the fingers the really tough fighters in the game, and there really isn't a tough bodychecker among them."

Someone with a skimpy knowledge of the game might accuse Richard of mouthing sour grapes. But there was truth in everything he said. Anyone who had seen the Rocket skating on "The Punch Line" with Toe Blake and Elmer Lach would affirm that.

"In my day," said Richard, "every team had at least one good line, and some of them had three good lines. Today, with fewer good players, every club changes the players around constantly, like parts in a machine. That hurts the quality of the game because the players don't get a chance to work exclusively with two other men and develop the pretty plays that come only through anticipating your linemates' moves.

"Then, there is the question of attitude. It has changed. Rivals on different teams are going into business with each other. I feel that all this fraternizing takes something off the competitive edge, and I know that when I played, fraternizing with the enemy was out."

Within three hours after I met Richard at the Mount Royal, I knew we had enough for a magazine article. I told him that I would write a complete story and then send him the manuscript for him to edit as he pleased. Following that,

I would return to Montreal, go over the corrections with him and we would be ready to publish.

I returned to Montreal in mid-summer with my wife, Shirley, and my friend, Ira Gitler, a longtime admirer of Richard who had never met him. Once again, I stayed at The Mount Royal Hotel and arranged to meet Richard for lunch in the main dining room. The Rocket was as gracious as ever—until the waiter arrived. He recognized Richard immediately but made the mistake of asking whether we wanted a round of Molson's beer. At that time the Molson family owned the Canadiens and, according to the Rocket, had treated him shabbily. What's more, Richard was doing some public relations work for Labatt's Beer. A trip-hammer exchange of French followed whereupon the waiter apologized profusely and returned with four bottles of Labatt's. The Rocket was smiling again.

He said he was pleased with my story and made very few alterations. I then asked Richard if he had ever considered writing a book. He told me that he once had been approached by a publisher who was to have a ghost writer work with him, but nothing had come of it. Yes, he said, he would be interested in doing a book with me. We agreed to wait until our magazine story hit the stands and then approach some publishers. We said our good-byes and agreed never to drink Molson's Beer again. I think the Rocket appreciated that as much as anything.

The article appeared in the November 1969 edition of *Sport* and was rewarded with a big cover line: "Hockey Was a Better Game in My Day" by Maurice Richard. It was a solid story and received a good deal of attention. Unbiased oldtimers applauded it, but those affiliated with expansion teams—including Lynn Patrick of the St. Louis Blues—criticized the Rocket for his "sour grapes" attitude.

Among those who were especially fond of the story was a very pleasant chap named Stuart Daniels. Daniels is a book

Ted Green (6) demonstrates why he was known as "Terrible Teddy." Here, as a member of the Bruins, he hits Wayne Mackie of the St. Louis Blues on the head with his stick during an exhibition game in September 1969. Mackie returned the favor. Green, shown sprawled on the ice, his face contorted, went to the hospital with a fractured skull. *(UPI)*

Guess who in his 1951 roller-hockey uniform.

Some of my first subjects as a hockey writer. Rangers goalie Gump Worsley withstands a Chicago onslaught in December 1956.

Phil Esposito, Boston's high-scoring center, is many things to many critics, but he's always hell on goaltenders.
(Mel DiGiacomo)

Esposito's hold on the Hart (most valuable player) Trophy was broken in 1972-73 by young, somewhat toothless Bobby Clarke, the gifted center and captain of the Philadelphia Flyers.
(Joel Bernbaum)

The possibility of a good fight always lures fans, and the Philadelphia Flyers, above, usually oblige. Hence their nicknames—The Mean Machine, The Broad Street Bullies. Here, they seem like dancers, frozen in a brawl with the Canadiens. But they weren't; it cost 58 minutes in penalties for all concerned. Opposite top, Boston's Bobby Orr (4) and New York's Brad Park (2), considered the two best defensemen in hockey, battle it out. Bottom, St. Louis Blues' Christian Bordeleau (21) cocks his stick at Vancouver Canucks' Pat Quinn (3). Below, Pete Mahovlich of Montreal (left) and Keith Magnuson of Chicago exchange blows. *(UPI, Dan Baliotti, UPI, UPI)*

If ever there was a "different" hockey player, it's Ken Dryden, the Montreal Canadiens goaltender. A lawyer, member of Ralph Nader's Raiders, and now president of the NHL Players' Association; not to mention member of the Stanley Cup champs in 1971 and 1973. Here Dryden has just stopped a shot by Red Wing Guy Charron. *(UPI)*

One man made the World Hockey Association a credible major league—Bobby Hull (left), the former Golden Jet of Chicago. Hull signed a multimillion-dollar deal with the WHA's Winnipeg Jets and won the league's most valuable player award (naturally) in 1972-73. *(Mel DiGiacomo)*

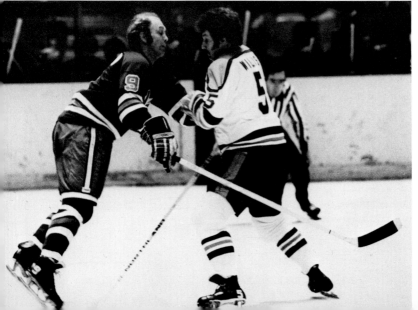

Bruin star Bobby Orr after a long drink from the Stanley Cup. The Bruins had defeated the Rangers 3-0 to win the Cup in six games during the 1972 playoffs. *(UPI)*

Things weren't quite so jolly in 1973, as Orr and teammate Phil Esposito sit glumly on the sidelines during their playoff series with the Rangers. They lost the series and never got near the Cup. *(UPI)*

Brad Park of the Rangers plays defense with a distillation of artistry . . . and anger *(Dan Baliotti)*

But Park is forever losing his shirt. Left, linesman Pat Shetler orders him to pick up his jersey and leave the ice after a fracas with Montreal's Ted Harris in 1969. Right, a year later, Shetler sends Park (already clutching jersey) off again. This time the foe was Bill Lesuk of Philadelphia. *(UPI)*

packager. He puts together books for publishers and then the publishers follow through with the printing, publishing and distribution. I had worked on Rod Gilbert's book, *Goal! My Life On Ice,* for Daniels, who had sold it to Hawthorn. Like myself, Daniels was fascinated with the Rocket and said he would like to assemble a Richard book. I put him in touch with Richard, and in almost no time at all we all agreed to terms.

The book was to be divided in half. One half would be a definitive history of the Montreal Canadiens; the other would be the Rocket's own story. We decided to call it *The Flying Frenchmen.* To compile Richard's portion of the book, I arranged to meet him for taping sessions at The Mount Royal. We now would be dealing with the Rocket's life from his early childhood memories right up to the present. We did the taping the following winter and I came away with a deep feeling of sadness about the man. By now, he had become so embittered toward the Canadiens' management that he rarely went to the Forum to see a game. But he still loved to play hockey and belonged to the Montreal team in the NHL Oldtimers Group. Every week the Rocket, heavy though he was, skated out wearing his old number nine. He allowed that he sometimes worried about overexertion. "Because the public always expects me to be the way I was ten or twenty years ago," he said, "I always try a bit too hard. I know they come to see me and I have my pride, so I try to be the way I was when I was twenty-five."

A younger member of the Oldtimers told Ted Blackman of the Montreal *Gazette* that watching Richard was a nerve-racking experience. "Sometimes," the player said, "they really go at it. Many of them, especially Richard, still have the basic skills, but they haven't got the legs. In one game, I made four passes from the corner to the Rocket. They were in the net so fast...."

Richard was more modest than ever. He said it was easy

for him to score with younger players on his line. "I just trail them up the ice and score five goals."

Richard told me that if business allowed he tried to play hockey four times a week. That, I said, sounded like more hockey than he played when he skated for the Canadiens. He laughed. "Most of the time," he said, "these are friendly games. I don't work as hard as I do when I'm playing in front of an audience. When the people are watching I try too hard. That's dangerous."

The book was published in January 1971. Richard was invited to New York for a promotion tour, although Daniels and I wondered just how much appeal the old warrior would have. It didn't take long to find out. Every radio and television sportscaster pleaded to have him on. When the Rocket attended an autographing session at Gerry Cosby's sporting goods store in Madison Square Garden, the place was jammed. "We've had autographing sessions before," said Michael Cosby, the store's manager, "but never a turnout like the one for the Rocket. It seemed like there were an awful lot of people who once had booed him and now wanted to come back and tell Richard just how much they admired him as a player."

Richard took it all in stride, then flew to Toronto where the Canadian publishers invited sixteen sports writers to the Royal York Hotel for coffee and croissants at 10 in the morning. Perhaps the best description of Rocket Richard, author, was provided by Alan Walker, who covered the "do" for *The Canadian Magazine:*

"He sat right on the edge of the couch, shoulders slung ahead, as a portly man will, his blue sports coat containing the paunch...His hair is grey now, and slicked down with Vitalis...His false top teeth are expensive, and so look real. His eyes, which used to be piercing enough to terrorize opposition goaltenders into helpless rigidity, now look smaller because his face has fattened."

That evening, The Rocket played in another Oldtimers Game at Maple Leaf Gardens. There were 15,279 spectators in the stands, many of whom remembered Richard when he set seventeen records in the NHL over an eighteen-season, 1,111-game career. Although it was a game against the Toronto Oldtimers, the Montreal players took it relatively humorously and announcer Jack Dennett helped by announcing some "special rules." Dennett said there would be no slapshots or bodychecking. "The penalties will be assessed on merit," he said. (Later Dennett gave Pete Conacher a twenty-second penalty for "tripping a 53-year-old man"—Buddy O'Connor.)

As expected, Richard received the biggest ovation when he was introduced as "the most famous, dynamic, explosive player—the man who rewrote the record book." Toronto won the game, 8-4, but Richard didn't seem overly perturbed. He had scored a goal and had been given a twenty-second penalty in the third period "for missing an open net." It was like old times in the dressing room after the game. Scores of media types surrounded the Rocket, and he answered their questions. But an hour later the star dust disappeared, and he headed back to Montreal where he had to tend to his jobs. Richard has his own company, General Fishing Lines, Ltd., and also works for S. Albert and Co. Ltd., a fuel company, He told me that he handles his fishing line enterprise in the basement den of his house. At Albert he heads a sales staff and occasionally helps clinch a deal for one of his men. "My name," said the Rocket, "still means something."

Some observers have commented on the tragedy of Richard's life in the Seventies, and told how he sits in his basement labeling eighteen dozen spools of line an hour, packs them into cardboard boxes and personally delivers them throughout hamlets in Quebec and Northern Ontario. But the Rocket I had worked with was a very simple man.

91

There was none of the high-pressure aura that modern players give off, and if Rocket-watchers wanted to feel sorry for him, he didn't particularly care.

"I have a good life now," he said. "I go fishing. I play tennis. I still play some hockey. I do what I want and go where I want to go, and even though a lot of people have forgotten me, I'm still asked for my autograph in a lot of places."

In October 1971 I dined with Neil Shayne, who then was hoping to place a World Hockey Association team in New York. Shayne asked if I thought the Rocket would be interested in managing his club, and I told him that a phone call would provide the answer. Richard sounded as amiable as ever when I phoned. "I'm not so sure about this new League," he said. "It would take quite a bit for me to move at my age."

Shayne eventually dropped out of the World Hockey Association picture, but the Rocket didn't. In July 1972 he signed with the Quebec Nordiques as coach. At long last the Rocket was to get his chance behind the bench. It didn't last long. After two games, Richard began suffering from nervous exhaustion. It was obvious that he couldn't handle the tension of the modern game, and a week later he handed in his resignation. "It's just too much," he said.

VII

THE LARRY ZEIDEL
STICK-SWINGING
ANTI-SEMITIC INCIDENT

As a Jew and a hockey fan, I always had made a point of checking the rosters of every professional and amateur team each season to determine whether any players of Hebrew extraction were making stickhandling their profession. I did this in the hopes of convincing my parents that I did, in fact, have a chance to become a professional hockey player myself and there was a method to my mad practice of executing a goaltender's splits on the living room floor.

My probe was rather disillusioning at first. I learned that the New York Rangers once had a player they touted as being "a Jewish goalie." They claimed that his name was Lorne Chabotsky, which sounded Hebrew enough. Later, however, I learned that Chabotsky's real name was Chabot, and he was as French-Canadian as pea soup and no more Jewish than the Pope.

Then came the uplifting news. The National Hockey League's Hart Memorial Trophy, given annually to the most valuable player, was donated to the NHL by Dr. David A. Hart, who was a Jew. His son, Cecil Hart, became

93

manager-coach of the Canadiens. In time I discovered that other Jews had made it to the top. Alex "Kingfish" Levinsky starred for the Toronto Maple Leafs and Chicago Black Hawks in the Thirties, and Hymie Buller emerged as one of the New York Rangers best defensemen in the early Fifties. Unfortunately, Buller arrived on the scene a bit too late to help my cause. It already had been determined that I would not become a professional hockey player, so my interest in Buller was purely that of a spectator and, of course, a fan.

Rooting for the Rangers in those days was as depressing as cheering for the French Army in 1940. They were a hapless outfit that inevitably finished out of the playoffs. What made them even more pathetic was their obvious lack of unadulterated fight. It was clear that if any team could be pushed around it was the Rangers, the ninety eight-pound weaklings of the NHL.

Buller, of course, became one of the patsies. He was a strong, smooth skater with a Mark Spitzian physique. Hymie could play a physical game, but by nature he was always clean. Playing for the non-belligerent Rangers, therefore, he was susceptible to intimidation. Just how much his Jewishness made Buller a target is debatable. The Rangers played up the ethnic angle as much as possible, and, inevitably, huge banners emblazoned with the star of David appeared hanging over the balcony of Madison Square Garden during Ranger home games. "Hymie," said one fan who subscribed to all Garden matches, "is not just a hockey player; he's *a Jew hockey player,* and we'll never let him forget it!"

This was no problem during the 1951-52 season when Buller's classy play at defense made him the talk of the league. His point total diminished a season later, but he played all seventy games on the league schedule and appeared destined to spend many more years in the majors.

But an incident early in the 1953-54 season virtually

destroyed Buller as an effective player in the NHL. The Rangers were host to the Detroit Red Wings, then the strongest team in hockey. They were to finish first by a country mile that year and annex the Stanley Cup. The Detroit sextet was as mean and nasty as it was good. Led by truculent Ted Lindsay, they would as soon jab the point of their stick in an enemy's belly as fire the puck into the net.

On this night the Rangers were putting up their usually futile defense against the champions and rapidly earned the visitors' disdain. During one exchange at center ice Buller checked Lindsay as cleanly as if the block was thrown by the Ivory Soap wrapper baby. The Detroit troublemaker rebounded from the check and skated directly at Buller. With two hands gripping the end of his stick, Lindsay whipped it around as if he were swinging a baseball bat. The gesture of intimidation was not unlike that of a Wild West gunfighter, scaring his enemy by firing a shot over his head. Lindsay had put Buller on notice.

Many of us in the crowd said a quick prayer which hopefully would give Hymie the strength to swing back. But nothing happened. Lindsay swung again, just barely missing Buller's head. This time the Ranger skated away. To the 12,000 or so witnesses it was the ultimate capitulation of the Jew to the *goy*. In the moralistic sense, Buller perhaps did the right thing. He did not involve himself in what would have been a vicious head-hunting affair in which blood inevitably would have been spilled and severe penalties meted out. He played it clean to the hilt and, as a result, was humiliated in the eyes of Ranger followers. Whether it was because of the Lindsay episode or not, Buller, who had been on the All-Star Team only two years earlier, bowed out of the NHL at the end of the season and never played in the majors again.

One who certainly blamed Buller for not hitting back was Larry Zeidel, another Jewish defenseman playing at the time. When Buller retired, Zeidel held the distinction of being the only Jew in professional hockey. That fact of life never eluded him. "When you're the only Jew in this bloody game," said Zeidel, "you have to prove you can take the rough stuff more than the average player." A former teammate of Lindsay's on the Red Wings, Zeidel practiced what he preached and became involved in an "anti-Semitic" incident because he *did* hit back.

I had never gotten to know Buller very well when he played for New York. At the time I was still at college and lacked the credentials necessary to interview a player. But by 1963 I was working for the *Journal-American* and I knew of Larry Zeidel and he knew of me. I felt that one day I must interview Larry the way other Jews believe that it is their destiny to someday visit Israel.

During the summer of 1963, I went on a week-long bicycle trip through the Pennsylvania-Dutch country. Larry was living in Hershey, so I decided that I would arrange to meet him at one of the youth hostels near his home. He agreed to visit me in the farm village of Denver, Pennsylvania, where our group was lodging for a couple of nights. Larry said he would drive over after work and I looked forward to the meeting with enormous anticipation.

Our hostel was located on a hill overlooking the long, winding road on which Zeidel would be traveling and I spent a half-hour trying to guess what kind of car he would be driving. My conclusion was that it would be a three-year-old Rambler station wagon since he was then playing in the minors, had a lot of children, and after all, was a hockey player. And every hockey player I had known was rather frugal.

Larry arrived in a brand-new Lincoln Continental. Right then and there I knew that this guy had class. He was warm and pleasant but the trademarks of his profession were obvious and ugly to the eye. Scars ran like a railroad map up and down his face, the legacy of a fractured skull, two concussions, a nose broken a dozen times and a collection of miscellaneous wounds worth more than 300 stitches. "Hockey is a game of survival of the fittest," said Zeidel. "Being a Jew I learned the ground rules for surviving earlier than most kids and it's helped me out ever since."

He was smaller than I had thought, but his five-feet-eleven, 185-pound frame seemed to be 98 per cent muscle. He said that he was raised in the rough Park Extension area of Montreal. The Zeidels were the only Jewish family in the neighborhood, and the neighbors punched home that bit of information whenever they could. "I got my first taste of anti-Semitism when I started school," he recalled. "The kids knew I was a Jew. They'd gang up on me. First it was one giant, then another."

He survived and he developed his own Jungle Rule Book, which ultimately was invoked on the hockey rink. By the early Fifties he had been acknowledged as one of the roughest players in *any* league. According to Zeidel, this was merely transference of his policy adopted on the streets of Montreal.

"A psychiatrist could have fun with me," said Zeidel. "He'd say I got that tough on account of having to fight for my rights as a Jew. It makes sense when you think of it. I figured that if I beat up the leader of the class gang, I'd be in good shape. I kept doing this through public school, and pretty soon I got a reputation and they left me alone. When I got into hockey I thought I'd use the same technique. I'd go for the bullies who'd try to run me outta the game and let them have it."

Zeidel's strategy worked in his youthful days, especially when he graduated to the hard-nosed Quebec League and later the Western League. Faceless voices in the crowds would taunt him and, occasionally, the players would deliver a barb or two themselves. "They might call me a 'Goddamn Jew' in a fit of anger," said Zeidel.

Often such taunts produced catastrophic results. While playing for Edmonton in 1952-53, Zeidel clashed with Jack Evans, an equally rugged defenseman for Saskatoon. Each broke his stick over the other's head; then they went on to engage in a bloody jousting exhibition that is regarded as one of the goriest in hockey history. It was the type of incident that the more temperate Hymie Buller always seemed to avoid. That, according to Zeidel, was Buller's biggest mistake.

"If Buller had belted those guys when they belted him, he'd have been a real star for years," said Zeidel. "He had a lot of finesse, a lot of ability, but he always acted like a gentleman. You can't do that in this game. He shouldn't have taken all the rough stuff they gave him. I know I wouldn't have."

Zeidel's words remained with me long after our meeting. I began following his career more closely and we soon became good friends. He eventually moved on to Seattle and then to Cleveland when, at the age of thirty-nine, he appeared near the end of his professional career. That was in the summer of 1967, the year that the NHL expanded from six to twelve teams. The *Journal-American* had folded in 1966 and I then was the Toronto *Star's* New York correspondent covering everything as well as continuing to write hockey pieces for various media. Larry had been doing well as a stockbroker, and I expected that he would pack up his skates once and for all and retire to the brokerage.

One afternoon in August 1967 I received a phone call from Zeidel. "I'm gonna try to get back into the NHL," he said.

"You're crazy," I replied. "You're too old. Nobody would go near you, expansion or not."

"Listen," he shot back, "I looked at those NHL draft picks and I had to laugh. I'm better than half the guys they've selected. How do I know? Well, I've played against 'em, that's how I know! Take a guy like Jean Ratelle of the Rangers. He's a first-rate NHL center, right? When I played against him three years ago, I could handle him; so I could do it now."

I thought it best to humor Larry with my silence and hope that he purged himself of any crazy thoughts about making it back to the NHL. That was the last time I underestimated him. After we had hung up Larry visited a doctor who determined that Zeidel had the heart of a twenty-year-old. He then obtained testimonials from various medical and hockey people endorsing his ability and fitness to play big-league hockey.

A few weeks after we had talked Larry phoned again. "I know you won't believe this," he said, bubbling over with enthusiasm, "but I've put together a first-class Madison Avenue brochure touting me as a potential NHL defenseman. I'm going to send it to all the teams. Whaddya think?"

"I admire your *chutzpah*—that's what I think."

"Well, nothing ventured, nothing gained. Let's see what happens."

Out of twelve tries, Zeidel obtained eleven rejections. The twelfth reply came from the Philadelphia Flyers. Zeidel was invited to training camp. Within two weeks he had made the team, and by the beginning of November the Flyers were sitting atop the West Division.

Zeidel had become a big-league celebrity at age thirty-nine. "You gotta think positive—think positive," he'd tell the younger players and often would give them a copy of *Psychocybernetics: A New Way to Get More Living Out of Life* by Dr. Maxwell Maltz.

It was becoming a glorious season for Larry, except for one disturbing aspect. The Boston Bruins, armed with the

99

toughest collection of skaters in contemporary hockey, appeared to some observers to have zeroed in on Zeidel and were battering him more than other Philadelphia skaters whenever the clubs met. This put Larry in a very difficult position since he had adopted a "turn-the-other-cheek" attitude with the Flyers. General Manager Bud Poile and coach Keith Allen remembered Zeidel's minor league outbursts and insisted that he not take "cheap" penalties. Larry interpreted this as a warning not to play "wild" hockey and therefore skated with a calm that belied his reputation as a bad man.

The Flyers high command was delighted. Philadelphia had a firm hold on first place, and even though a leak in the roof of the Spectrum arena had forced the Flyers to play "home" games on the road, they had a remarkable *esprit de corps* that sustained their momentum. Larry, of course, was the leader.

On March 7, 1968, the Flyers played another of their "home" games at Maple Leaf Gardens in Toronto. Facing them were "the Big, Bad Bruins." With such truculent skaters as Ted Green, Ken Hodge, Johnny McKenzie and Eddie Shack, the Boston club specialized in a policy of victory by intimidation.

This night was no different. "The Bruins," wrote Rex MacLeod of the Toronto *Globe and Mail,* "brutally effective with bodychecks, wore down the Flyers with a discouraging barrage." Once again, Zeidel appeared to be a prime target. One theory had it that there actually was a Bruins plot to "get" Zeidel for whatever reasons. Forbes Kennedy, a former Bruin playing for Philadelphia, reportedly heard about it from his onetime teammates and mentioned this to manager Poile before the opening face-off. According to some sources, Poile alerted referee Bob Sloan, who ignored the warning.

"We know," said Poile, "that the Bruins warned Larry they were going to get him. It was more than just idle baiting you hear in most sports."

No sooner had the teams taken the ice for the opening period when Zeidel found himself in trouble. Derek Sanderson of the Bruins was standing in front of the Flyers net when a shot headed for the goal. "I was going to tip it in," Sanderson told me later. "but Zeidel stuck out his stick and tipped it so it caught me at the bottom of my eye. The puck ripped the skin wide open and I was knocked flat to the ice." Sanderson was taken to the Gardens' hospital and the game continued, developing a new crescendo of hatred with every rush up and down the ice.

As the overhead clock ticked past the nine-minute mark, Zeidel again skated onto the ice along with Eddie Shack, a player with whom he had engaged in a stick-swinging duel a decade earlier. Within seconds the white-jerseyed Shack and the orange-jerseyed Zeidel were face-to-face, swinging sticks at each other's head, and frequently connecting. Zeidel opened a wound on the back of Shack's head while Shack sliced open Zeidel's forehead. The two continued their duel until it wound up behind the Flyers' goal before linesmen intervened and referee Sloan banished both of them from the game with match penalties.

Superficially, it appeared to be another in a long line of Zeidel clashes, no different than his set-to with Jack Evans or his previous episode with Shack. "I was only a rookie at the time of our first battle," said Shack. "Zeidel speared me twice and I said 'spear me again and I'll hit you right over the head.' He speared me again so I let him have it, right over the head."

Yet, it seemed strange that Larry, who so desperately wanted to remain in the NHL, would depart from his new policy of quasi-pacifism—unless he was unreasonably provoked. At noon the next day I received a phone call from Marie Zeidel, Larry's wife. She was near tears as she explained the gist of a telephone conversation she had had with her husband. According to Mrs. Zeidel, Larry *had* been unreasonably provoked.

She recounted how her husband had been taunted with anti-Semitic remarks by not one or two but several Boston players. "This," she insisted, "isn't the normal run of hockey fighting. This is plain evil."

After listening to Marie Zeidel spell out the charges against the Boston players, I asked her just what she had hoped to accomplish. Marie said that she wanted the story exposed to public view. I told her that the most I could do would be to phone my sports editor, Milt Dunnell of the Toronto *Star*. In the meantime, I wanted Marie to put me in touch with Larry who was enroute to Quebec City with the Flyers.

I phoned Dunnell, perhaps the most insightful and competent sports editor there ever was and certainly the most pleasant to work with, and explained the gist of Marie Zeidel's message. By now, the *Star* was approaching its last deadline for the late edition and there was little room for a large story. Dunnell decided to run Marie's statement in a "box" of two or three paragraphs and follow-up with a comprehensive story the following day, Saturday, March 9, 1968.

In the meantime NHL President Clarence Campbell had ordered Zeidel and general manager Bud Poile to appear at league headquarters for a hearing on the stick-swinging incident. Late on Friday afternoon I contacted Larry and he related his side of the story. He said that members of the Bruins had been taunting him with slurs such as "Jew boy, we're goin' to put you in the gas chamber." I immediately cut in and warned him that this was tough stuff. If it hit the papers, I said, there would be quite a bit of flak in Boston,

Montreal and Philadelphia—and that was just for starters.

"There's no point pulling any punches." Larry insisted. "I want to bring out everything. Everything!"

Zeidel reiterated that he had gone out of his way to "turn the other cheek" and reminded me that his penalty minute total was relatively low. But, he went on, the anti-Jewish slurs had provoked him beyond his control. "When they say 'Jew boy' and go into that gas chamber business, they're on sensitive ground. My parents are from the old country. My grandparents were burned to death in concentration camps—wiped out! I can't live with myself, listening to that abuse and turning my cheek."

To my surprise, Larry insisted that Shack, of all people, be absolved of blame. He did single out such Bruins as Ted Green, Don Awrey, Gerry Cheevers and Tom Williams. He revealed that the tormenting had begun on January 4, 1968, when Awrey took a "good run at me." Larry elaborated:

"I gave him the elbow and the lumber. But I went easy on the kid. I could have really given it to him. Now here's the joke. This bad man of the NHL, leading the league in penalties, this paper tiger, went and told his daddy (Ted Green). It's comical. Green gave me a spear in the face and knocked me into the net so hard I thought I'd come out the other side. And all the time I told myself, 'I gotta keep cool.' But when we got to Toronto, I had a feeling something was going to happen.

"In our locker room before the game, when all we should have been thinking about was the game, the guys on our team were all concerned. They were saying things like 'Don't worry, Larry, we'll protect you.' I had to get up and make a speech. I told 'em, 'It's up to you guys. I can play it cool and turn the other cheek. Just play your regular game.' "

I wasn't certain whether Zeidel realized the ramifications of his statements. He was talking for the record, knowing

103

that what he was saying would make headlines in the Toronto *Star,* Canada's largest-selling newspaper, and soon would be gobbled up by every newspaper in every NHL city.

I had mixed emotions. On the one hand, I experienced the typical newsman's reflex over a potentially big story. This was a scoop and the adrenalin had been flowing since my conversation with Marie Zeidel. On the other hand, I was concerned about Zeidel and what the Establishment would do to him for calling a slur a slur—in public. Obviously, Larry had taken as much as he possibly could take.

"I've been playing like a choir boy this season," he went on. "I'm like a three-time loser; I know I can't win at this game. There comes a point where maybe you have to throw away the psychology books. You have to live with yourself. Sometimes it's bad for morale on a team if a player runs away."

What made Zeidel's accusations that much more potent was the fact that he named names on the Bruins. He recalled a moment when Shack checked him into the boards directly in front of the Bruins bench. "I looked up," said Larry, "and there were cheerleaders going at it. There was big bad man Don Awrey and Tommy Williams sitting on the bench having fun like a couple of delinquents. Then Gerry Cheevers joined the band."

Sure enough, the story ran as the lead item on the front page of the Toronto *Star's* sports section on Saturday, March 9, 1968. " 'JEW BOY' SLURS INFLAME ZEIDEL."

The newspapers hit the stands in Toronto at just about the time Zeidel and Poile walked into Campbell's Montreal office. Poile insisted that the alleged anti-Semitic slurs be discussed at the meeting, but Campbell refused to allow testimony on them, ruling that they had no connection with the fight since Zeidel emphatically absolved Shack of making anti-Semitic remarks. "Shack," Zeidel later explained, "was on the ice like the big enforcer."

Campbell fined both players $300 apiece and suspended Zeidel for four games and Shack for three. However, the league president allowed that he would conduct a separate investigation of the alleged slurs. "The Boston club," said Campbell, "will have to answer for any accusation made."

Before the weekend was over the shit had hit the fan in Boston. Bob Sales, whom I had known as a very competent reporter with the defunct New York *Herald-Tribune,* was covering the story for the Boston *Globe.* His story appeared more explosive than my original. The six-column headline in the *Globe* said it all: "ZEIDEL CALLS 3 BRUINS ANTI-SEMITIC." The subhead mentioned the "gas chamber" remark and cited Cheevers, Awrey and Williams. A second subhead was even more potent, since Bruins coach Harry Sinden was mentioned. It said: "SINDEN CONCEDES SLURS, BUT SEES NO BIGOTRY."

Personally, I had expected the Bruins to deny everything, but Sinden's statement to Sales was a revelation. The coach put it this way to the Boston reporter: "I didn't hear any of it, but I don't doubt that somebody called him a Jew boy, or something like that. Guys are always taunting each other. That doesn't mean they're bigots. I've heard guys call Phil Esposito a wop. We call Tom Williams a stupid American."

Sinden, who had a reputation for being one of the more intelligent people in hockey management, then zeroed in on Zeidel's weak spot in the case. "You know," Sinden added, "when you sit in judgment you have to take into consideration the man's reputation. He's one of the all-time stickmen in the game. He's also a man who's been known to prepare his case very well in the past."

By Monday afternoon Zeidel didn't know whether to keep talking or shut his mouth altogether. His reaction depended upon the particular interviewer. "I'm supposed to be lying low on this thing," he told George Sullivan of the Boston *Herald-Traveler*. "I don't want to rake up the coals."

Then, he read an article about *The Rise and Fall of the Third Reich*, which had been made into a television film. Once again he was aroused. "They said they made the film to remind the American population of the madness that once was inflicted on mankind," said Zeidel, "and that it could happen again. That must be prevented.

"If they call you a dirty Jew, or something like that, so what? They say the same kinds of things about Frenchmen. It's the violent world of hockey, right? Trying to shake you up verbally to break up your concentration is all part of the game. But when they start saying things like we'll carry you out on a slab and send you to the gas chamber, and there's an enforcer on the ice trying to lay you out, that's another thing."

The question now was what Campbell would do. Knowing the NHL hierarchy and its abhorrence of negative publicity, I was certain that he would somehow try to defuse the controversy. His best stratagem, as I saw it, would be to approach Ed Snider, president of the Flyers and a Jew, and attempt to dissuade him from pursuing the Zeidel case.

Meanwhile, I decided to contact the B'nai B'rith Anti-Defamation League and the American Jewish Committee. Both organizations immediately launched their own probes. I also phoned A. Alan Borovoy, director of the Canadian Labor Committee for Human Rights. After studying the news stories, Borovoy blasted Sinden for his rationale that appeared in the Boston *Globe*. "Racist invective," said Borovoy, "does not qualify as good-natured needling. It should be clearly stated, from the league president to the custodian of the locker room, that anti-Semitic, anti-ethnic insults have no place in the NHL. Any player who engages in them or any official who condones them should be disciplined by the league officialdom."

Enough non-hockey officials had now gotten into the act to compel Campbell to take decisive action. The issue hinged on the Flyers themselves. I phoned Ed Snider later in the week to determine just what his position would be on the matter. He didn't immediately return my call, but when I finally did hear from him I got the message, quiet and clear. In a wishy-washy statement, Snider indicated that the Flyers were not going to pursue the matter. Bud Poile, who had seemed so emphatically in support of Zeidel during the days after the episode, suddenly took a new stance. The Philadelphia organization began to pressure Zeidel to drop the charges. Then, on Wednesday, March 13, 1968, Campbell made a rather surprising announcement. "I don't intend to let it drop. The allegations were made."

Meanwhile, the Flyers made a gallant run to the finish line and captured first place in the West Division, ironically winning the Clarence Campbell Bowl. Zeidel, even more ironically, was a star in the championship drive. The start of the Stanley Cup playoffs distracted everybody from the Zeidel case, which was well and good for the NHL executives. However, a behind-the-scenes probe continued. Two non-Jewish fans who had been sitting behind the Bruins' bench on the night of the incident wrote letters to Campbell and said that they had heard anti-Semitic obscenities hurled at Zeidel by Bruins players. The Toronto *Telegram* also ran a story that supported Zeidel.

Nothing was heard from Campbell until the playoffs were over. I encountered him at a league governors' meeting in New York City. "I have something that will interest you," he told me. "You are concerned with the Zeidel case; well, here is my decision." I read it carefully. All things considered it was a brilliant whitewash of a very dirty subject, conceived, I'm sure, with the cooperation of the

Flyers' hierarchy and other interested parties. Campbell did acknowledge that Bruins players had called Zeidel "Jew" or "Jewish." He then went on to say:

"The use of abusive remarks or gestures as part of the baiting or needling of opposing players in sports is contemptible at any time. This is something which all sports can do without and recently some very heavy fines have been imposed against offenders in this League. We are prepared to take even more stringent measures to stamp it out. It contributes nothing to the playing of the game itself and is highly offensive to those who hear it whether they are opposing players or spectators.

"It can be stated with certainty that there is no anti-racial or anti-religious feeling or other form of discrimination of any kind in this league at any level of participation—from players to the owners—and none will be tolerated. Any time it appears, it will be dealt with severely."

Campbell did not deny that the Bruins had bombarded Zeidel with a variety of abusive terms "in the same way as some of their teammates were referred to as "Wops" or "Dagos" or "Ukes" or "Micks." Thus, the Bruins insisted that in referring to Zeidel in this manner they were not anti-Semitic or anti-anybody. It was simply an allusion to a fact extensively publicized by Zeidel himself when he was seeking employment as a player during the previous summer and fall, added Campbell.

The Flyers also failed to carry the puck for their defenseman. "Lacking any evidence in support of Zeidel's original charges," said Campbell, "by reason of his own refusal to provide any verification or support of them, they [the charges] have not been proven. His motivation for making them can only be speculated upon as he declined to cooperate in their investigation."

To cap his statement, Campbell alluded to letters he had received in support of Zeidel. "These letters," Campbell concluded, "identified three Boston players. None of these letters referred to any expression associated with Nazi persecution of Jews. The players named in the letters and referred to by Zeidel in the stick-swinging inquiry and the team coach were interrogated and it was clearly established that the spectators' identification had been in error."

That was it. Zeidel wondered what effect the brouhaha would have on his career. He had played remarkably well for the Flyers, had obtained more positive publicity—aside from the Bruins episode—for the team than any other player and spent the summer of 1968 selling season tickets for the club.

When Larry reported to training camp in September 1968, he was in the best condition of his life and anticipating the new season with his usual *élan*. Bud Poile, however, had imported a couple of new defensemen and appeared less cordial to Larry than he had been the previous year. Unperturbed, Zeidel continued to drive as hard as he ever had, but this time it appeared that the Flyers were determined to keep him on the sidelines.

About a month after the season began, Poile asked Zeidel to report to the Flyers' farm team in Quebec City. Larry knew he was being railroaded and refused. "I believed that I was good enough to stay in the NHL," he said, "and my record proves it." Neither side budged, so Zeidel spent the remainder of the 1968-69 season on the sidelines. By no coincidence the Flyers faltered badly and failed to defend their championship successfully. In 1969 Larry retired from hockey and went into the investment counseling business. Poile was fired by Ed Snider that same year.

Zeidel became a successful broker, remaining in Philadelphia with his wife and family. He was the "color" commentator on radio for the Flyers during the 1971-72 season and has remained close to the Philadelphia hockey scene.

The case made its mark on all of us who were involved. Breaking the story, as I did, hardly endeared me to the Bruins, nor to some Boston hockey writers. Although a year later a member of the club's publicity department confessed to me in a weak moment that he believed there had been a "get" Zeidel brigade and that Ted Green had led it.

Nearly five years after Marie Zeidel phoned me to report the Bruins-anti-Semitism incident, I interviewed her again. I was curious about her reflections on the incident. Did she have any regrets about calling me? "No," Mrs. Zeidel replied, "I'm not sorry about a thing. Naturally, I've reflected on the whole business many times since 1968 and came to several conclusions. Perhaps the most important question is why did I call you in the first place?

"The thing that motivated me the most was the fact that I saw Larry and Shack and the stick-swinging on television and it looked so, so bad. I have to admit that I panicked a little. At first I thought that Campbell would overreact to the violence and bar Larry from hockey.

"More than that, I was concerned about what people would think about Larry if they didn't know the facts behind the case. They might think he was some raving maniac if they didn't know the reasons that moved him. Without such evidence it would be hard to justify Larry's action. Somebody had to come to Larry's defense, and that's why I phoned you."

Marie said that the incident was never discussed in their household. She admitted that she wasn't quite sure how Larry felt about it five years later. After interviewing Marie, I discussed the incident with Larry. As I had anticipated, he did not share his wife's view of the affair, but he did not appear bitter about it either.

"Sure I'm sorry about it," said Larry, "sorry about a lot of aspects of the thing. After all, I was an old war horse who had played pro hockey for twenty years, and my philosophy

110

always had been, 'If you can't stand the heat, stay out of the kitchen.'

"The trouble with Boston had been brewing for some time. It started the first time we played when I accidentally speared Don Awrey and it got really bad the second time; even before the game started. The Bruins were heckling me at center ice.

"My great regret is that I didn't strike back instantly; right then and there. Then, the tension wouldn't have built up. If it was the old Larry Zeidel I wouldn't have turned the other cheek but I kept thinking how Poile and Allen had kept telling me to stay cool and avoid penalties, so I was being too goddamn cute with the Bruins when I should have lashed back. So, my big mistake was not nipping the trouble right in the bud."

Larry admitted that he had many things on his mind. Because of his age, he had no bargaining power about his future despite his "plus-minus" figure (by which managers rate defensemen), plus-17, extraordinarily good for a defenseman on a brand-new team.

"I kept thinking about how other teams had rejected me in the past because I had had so many penalties and I wanted to do things the way the Flyers management wanted me to do them. But I knew what hockey was all about; how violent it could get. I said a lot of things but I was disappointed after the stories came out in the paper." What hurt Zeidel most was that the NHL had made it seem as if he was coming to Campbell for help, which, he claims was the last thing in the world on his mind. "What I did was apologize for my actions in the incident with Shack," Larry explained. "I didn't go crying to Campbell."

In retrospect, Zeidel allowed that the incident may have temporarily hurt the NHL's image There was little doubt that it had ended the Flyers love affair with him. "That summer after the incident," Zeidel remembered, "the team president, Bill Putnam, asked me to sell season tickets for the Flyers. Well, I agreed and then went out and brought in more goddamned dollars than they were paying me. I really felt good about the team and everything."

Then, of course, Poile benched him and finally ordered Larry back to the minors. "So," Zeidel said, "what was I supposed to think? I couldn't put my finger on it and say, yeah, it was the Bruins business that caused this. I felt like a pitcher who had won 20 games one year and was in the bullpen as a fourth-string reliever before the new season even started." I asked Larry what he would have done if he could live the Bruins episode over again. "When I play it all back in my head," he said, "I realize that I was too goddamned cute. If I'd been the Larry Zeidel of the tough Park Extension neighborhood of Montreal, none of this would have happened!"

VIII

ADVENTURES
WITH
GORDIE HOWE

My introduction to Gordie Howe came via those hockey broadcasts my miniscule Transitone picked up from Toronto and Montreal as if they were coming from across town. As a result I frequently listened to the crescendo-ing Foster Hewitt (Toronto) and Doug Smith (Montreal) relate the exploits of young Howe, who already had taken on a Bunyanesque image.

Unfortunately for me, as Howe reached his peak as a right wing with the Detroit Red Wings, I was a Toronto Maple Leaf fan and so my feelings toward him were decidedly hostile. They didn't change as I reached adulthood because I went to work for the New York Rangers, a club which Howe managed to destroy as easily as he crumpled the Leafs.

It wasn't until I began writing hockey for *The Hockey News* that I met Howe face-to-face. From time to time when the Red Wings played at Madison Square Garden I would visit the Detroit dressing room after a match. Any hostility I might have harbored earlier toward Gordie was quickly extinguished by his calm, laconic style and frequent words of good humor.

113

These, however, were casual encounters. In the fall of 1960 I had my first real meeting with Howe. Al Silverman, then managing editor of *Sport* magazine, asked me to work with Gordie on an article called "Nobody Can Knock Hockey to Me." It would carry Howe's byline and I think there was around $500 in it for him, which in those days was not bad for doing very little. All Gordie had to do was meet me one afternoon at the Roosevelt Hotel in Manhattan and go over a list of anti-hockey "knocks," which he then would topple. I was suitably nervous before the meeting, wondering just how the Great Man would treat me, a relatively young reporter on the beat. I arrived at the hotel punctually at 2 P. M. and Howe was there sitting in the lobby. He was cordial, if not warm, and treated the questions as methodically as he would an opponent trying to skate past him. Each "knock" was intercepted and converted to a "boost" for the game.

My uneasiness never quite left me, perhaps because I sensed that Howe was somewhat impatient with the questions, although this may simply have been a manifestation of my own paranoia. But he was good in spots, particularly when he discussed that night in March 1950 when he lay near death in Detroit's Harper Hospital with a few yards of bandages wrapped around his head and a big, fat patch over his right eye—all a product of a collision with Ted Kennedy of the Maple Leafs. He admitted that that was the closest he ever came to quitting hockey. But strangely enough "despite the pain shooting up and down my body," he said, "I realized I was eager to get on the ice again, although I later spent much of the summer doubting if I could come back."

Then he told me about the time he played baseball months after the operation and saw two balls coming at him instead of one. His friends urged him to forget hockey, but he insisted on coming to the Red Wings training camp in the fall of 1950. "When I skated on the ice, I felt a little jittery," Gordie recalled, "but once I made it through the first practice, I knew I'd be okay. After a couple of games I felt better than ever and I continued to improve as I went along. I led the NHL in scoring that season for the first time, and I knew I had made the right decision in coming back. I knew then and I know now that I owe every good thing I've gotten out of life to hockey."

The interview concluded about a half-hour sooner than I had anticipated but I was determined to do *anything* to make the Great Man happy, even if it meant shortening our discussion. After all, the next important step was obtaining his approval of the written story.

Writing it was no sweat at all. Having been a hockey press agent myself and as deeply in love with *The* Game as Howe, I was able to refute all the knocks as ardently and more articulately than he could. Once into the piece, I pounded the typewriter as hard as Howe's skate would churn the ice on a breakaway. I finished the article in a couple of days, rewrote it once and then dispatched a copy to Gordie and another copy to Silverman at *Sport*. Then I held my breath for a week, awaiting Howe's reply. Would he rip the article apart and, conceivably, write me off as an author? Or would he approve the text that I felt reflected his views up and down the line?

The answer came eight days after the story was mailed to him. Gordie made about three minor changes, initialed his *"OK, Gordie Howe"* in the top left corner of the manuscript, and the story ran in the February 1961 issue of *Sport* with a bold cover line. Several sports columnists lifted excerpts from the piece, and I was quite relieved that a good job had been done. More important, that I had collaborated with a member of contemporary hockey's royalty. A month went by before the star dust cleared out of my eyes.

Sport magazine also was pleased with the piece, which,

in a way, was more important to me than Howe's approval. Silverman and his assistants Irv Goodman and Jack Zanger already had given me a number of hockey assignments. Usually, they were profile features, running about 3,000 words and requiring at the very least a one-hour face-to-face interview with the subject.

The first I ever did was on Andy Bathgate, then the hottest scorer on the Rangers. Later I wrote profiles of Glenn Hall, the Chicago Black Hawks goaltender, and Toronto Maple Leafs defenseman Carl Brewer, to name a couple. To those of us who wrote for *Sport,* the ultimate assignment was "The Sport Special," which was longer than the traditional profile and demanded longer interviews.

A "Special" could run as long as 10,000 words, sometimes more, and usually required that the author travel with his subject, at least for a day or two. In November 1963, Silverman phoned me and asked whether I'd like to do a "Special" on Gordie Howe. This was, if you'll forgive the expression, a special "Special" since Howe was on the verge of breaking Maurice Richard's NHL record of 544 goals. Not only would I be writing an in-depth article on Howe, I would—hopefully—be sitting in on and writing about hockey history in the making. It was an assignment made in heaven.

This time, however, Gordie was not as amenable as he had been the first time we had collaborated. He had just tied Richard's career goal record of 544 and the pressure had been great. The Red Wings' front office was reluctant to allow newsmen to bother him except for the usual post-game interviews. Fortunately, the Detroit general manager happened to be Sid Abel—once Howe's linemate on the famed "Production Line"—and one of the nicest men in hockey. Abel suggested I meet Howe at the Queen Elizabeth Hotel in Montreal on Friday evening, November 2, 1963, the night before the Red Wings were to play the Canadiens at Montreal's Forum.

According to the plan, I would spend Saturday with Howe, and then travel with the Red Wings after the game that night on their charter flight to Boston for a Sunday night game against the Bruins. Presumably, Howe would have scored his record-breaking goal by then and I would have one hell of a story.

Never having played in a Stanley Cup final, I cannot relate the rate of stomach churnings per minute experienced by a big-league hockey player but, to me, the upcoming meetings with Howe had great potential for excitement. Perhaps that's why I arrived at the Trans-Canada Terminal at Idlewild that Friday night a good three-quarters of an hour before my plane's departure time.

It was a miserable, rainy night in New York but not harsh enough to prevent normal flights out. When I boarded our Viscount prop-jet armed with my briefcase and sheaf of research material, I expected that we would take off on time. But, alas, we sat for more than a half-hour on the runway before the stewardess announced that there would be an undetermined delay before take-off.

I flipped out. This would surely screw up my rendezvous with Howe. I ran up to the stewardess and asked if I could leave the plane for a few moments to make a phone call. She agreed and I alighted along with about six other passengers who no doubt had appointments to cancel. I did not want to cancel my meeting with Howe, only set it back an hour or so because the encounter seemed very important in setting up the necessary rapport for our interview.

When I reached the Trans-Canada Terminal, a make-shift quonset hut, I discovered that all phones were tied up or inoperable. No matter. The stewardess had assured me that we would not take off for at least an hour. I dashed out of the terminal, turned left and ran toward the huge Pan American Terminal, about a quarter of a mile away. Surely, there would be ample telephones there.

I found the phones and tried to reach Howe. The hotel

operator said she was ordered not to put any calls through to his room. Would she take a message? Yes, but there was no guarantee that he would receive it. Getting desperate, I gave her the message that I would be delayed and then phoned Western Union and wired another message to Howe. That done, I dashed back to the Trans-Canada Terminal relieved that I had done everything possible to tell Gordie I'd be late.

As I headed for the runway, a large uniformed guard came darting out from behind the TCA desk and grabbed me by the right arm. "I'm afraid you can't go through that door," he said. "The plane to Montreal has already left."

"Already left!"

I'm sure my scream carried all the way to Montreal, if not to the lobby of the Queen Elizabeth Hotel.

"Don't be upset," he continued. "By the way, is your name Fischler?"

Between ʹattempts at fainting, I allowed that it was. "Well, sir," the TCA man went on, "you'll be happy to know that we managed to rescue your briefcase before the plane took off."

Alternately fuming and plotting how I would get the stewardess fired, I reclaimed my briefcase and learned that there would be another flight to Montreal in an hour. This time I vowed not to leave the cabin even if the plane remained stalled on the runway overnight. As it was, we departed on time and I arrived in the lobby of the Queen Elizabeth Hotel at about 10:30 p.m. Sid Abel was there and said that Gordie had been looking for me. He wouldn't be available on Friday night after all and instead wanted to meet me for breakfast on Saturday morning.

I met Howe in the dining room. He was accompanied by Billy McNeill, a blond, journeyman winger and a very congenial fellow. I was reminded that this was almost eighteen years to the day when Howe played his first professional hockey game in Omaha in November 1945.

Now, brown-eyed thirty-five-year-old Gordie, the best hockey player in the world for more than a decade, had sprinkles of gray hair mixed with brown at the temples. He appeared relaxed as he devoured his scrambled eggs and bacon, but I couldn't say the same for myself. I was self-conscious about having to trail around with him when it seemed that he wanted at least a bit of privacy. "No," he insisted, "we're going to take a walk over to the shopping center. C'mon along with us."

This was not necessarily a strategically sound move on Gordie's part. The *Place Ville Marie* shopping center was crowded, and many of the people were hockey fans who resented the fact that Howe soon would break their beloved Rocket's record.

"Hey, Gordie," a man in a Canadiens jacket snapped, "they're gonna check you real good tonight."

Howe, whose sloped shoulders tended to minimize his six-foot, 200-pound frame, grinned. "I suppose so," he said without hesitation, "but they shoulda thought of that 544 goals ago. Ay!"

Like many Canadians, he punctuated his sentences with an all-inclusive "ay." When a question required an explanation in depth, he drew out his words—like "awwfullll"—to give himself a chance to phrase it correctly. Sometimes he dragged them out so long he appeared to have a stammer. But he was sharp with a comeback and never missed blunting a verbal needle with a good punch line.

"Canadiens beat you bad last week," the pest said to Howe.

"Heck," Gordie said, "you know hockey. It's a game of mistakes. Our mistake was getting out of bed that morning."

I asked him if the fans ever embarrassed or annoyed him enough to make him want to crawl away through a manhole? "Awwww, no," he drawled, "that's just water off a duck's back. Only thing that bothers me is when somebody *won't* come up to me. They'll stay sorta far away and say: 'Look, there goes the big-shot.' Heck, I'm no big-shot."

Which was both true and not true. Obviously he was the biggest name in hockey. Yet, his modesty and affability was there for everyone to see. A middle-aged woman asked for his autograph, then assured him: "You'll score one tonight, Gordie."

He smiled: "Yeah, in practice."

A teenager approached him, stuck out a large scrapbook with a Red Wing symbol on the cover and asked Howe when he thought he'd score his next goal. "Sometime this year," Gordie said with a chuckle.

"Are you worried about it, Gordie?"

"I will be if I don't get it by March."

He walked past a music shop. The shop window was decorated with posters. One of them read: "Gordie Howe—recorded by Big Bob and the Dollars on Globe Records." Inside we could hear the throbbing rock beat and then the chorus:

Gordie Howe is the greatest of them all,
The greatest of them all,
Yes, the greatest of them all.
You can have your choice of all the rest,
If you're a Howe fan, you've got the very best.

The newsstand was filled with papers in both French and English. All of them headlined Howe's shot at Richard's record. He stopped and looked at the papers. "There's a lotta talk about my goals, but all I want now is to play two more years in this league. That'll give me twenty years up here, somethin' that's been my ambition for years. Only one other man has been able to do that—Dit Clapper of the Bruins. When I tie his record I will be the happiest man in the world."

He bought a chocolate bar. "If I can get more than twenty

years, I'd like to. Right now I think I can do it, providing I don't get a bad injury."

We walked back to the Queen Elizabeth hotel for the traditional afternoon pregame steak dinner. Gordie ordered eggs again. "They go down easier. Steak isn't *that* important. I once scored two goals on a couple of milk shakes when I was with Omaha."

After the meal, a girl in her twenties approached. "Mr. Howe," she said, "do you sign autographs?"

"Sure I do," he said as he wrote "Best of everything, Gordie Howe."

The girl smiled. "You know," she went on, "I'm from Newfoundland."

"Awww," Gordie kidded, "don't feel bad about it."

He then begged off to take his late afternoon pregame nap. When he woke up he hailed a cab for the ten minute drive to the Forum. Surprisingly, the capacity crowd seemed to be rooting for Howe, but he couldn't buy a goal. Later, on the Red Wings' charter flight to Boston after the game, Howe played cards in the back of the plane with Alex Delvecchio and Parker MacDonald. I sat next to defenseman Irv Spencer, whom I had known when he played for New York. It was a short flight and the plane touched down smoothly at Logan Airport. Just a few yards away, a chartered bus awaited the team.

The players filed in cracking jokes. Forward Larry Jeffrey pointed at Howe's droopy shoulders. "Gordie," he said, "you're the only guy in the league who keeps a permanent hanger in his suits to fill out the shoulders."

This time the Red Wings camped at the Hotel Kenmore. I arranged to meet Gordie at breakfast, and he was right on time. After the meal, we repaired to the lobby, which was bare compared to the Queen Elizabeth. It was easier for Gordie to relax. After some idle talk, he looked at his watch.

121

It was 11:30 A. M. He turned to teammate Parker Mac-Donald, tipped his head in the direction of the door, and the three of us got up for a walk.

It was dreadfully cold, and the bitter winds coming off the Charles River penetrated my heavy coat as we approached Fenway Park. Gordie got to talking about his semi-pro baseball days in Saskatchewan. "Back home," he said, "I once hit the longest ball you ever saw. It took off high between short and second. The second baseman drifted out on the grass for it. Then, one of our crazy winds came along and got hold of it. The pitcher called for it, then the catcher. Know something? That ball wound up in the parking lot behind the backstop. That's a Saskatchewan summer for you!"

When we returned to the hotel Gordie said he wanted to relax alone for a while. I met him again at 6 P. M. when the team gathered in the Kenmore lobby for the trip to Boston Garden for the game. I said a few prayers, hoping that Gordie would score at least a goal and then took off for the arena.

The Bruins were a mediocre sixth-place hockey club, but neither Gordie nor his teammates could do a thing right that night. Once again, he failed to get the record-breaking goal, and as a result the Detroit dressing room was filled with stifling tension after the game. I quickly said my good-byes and returned to New York.

As luck would have it, Howe scored his record-breaking goal a week later. I phoned him for details and he cooperated, as usual. Then, I sat down and wrote, or at least tried to write.

I was tighter than Howe trying to break Richard's record. This was not a simple piece like the earlier "Nobody Can Knock Hockey to Me." It required craftsmanship and plenty of time, and I labored over it for more than a week. When Silverman and the other editors at *Sport* finally read it, I again held my breath. Jack Zanger, my closest friend at the magazine, phoned. "It's the best piece you've ever done for us," he said. I thanked him, hung up, ran to the refrigerator and celebrated with a bottle of Coke and two · scoops of chocolate ice cream.

I had two gripes with the article once it hit the stands: first, as much as *Sport* liked it, they didn't feature it on the cover as they had the earlier Howe article; and second, the color photo accompanying the story was unusually blah. Otherwise I was delighted and the word from Detroit was that Gordie was pleased, too.

The Howe article established me as *the* hockey writer for *Sport.* Steve Gelman, who succeeded Al Silverman as managing editor, made it clear that I could have just about any hockey assignment I wanted.

IX

AT WAR WITH BOBBY ORR

There is no Bobby Orr. Sure, there is a phenomenon with a number four on it that skates around like nothing most of us have ever seen. Sure, there is a fair-haired vision in black and yellow and white who scores points and wins games and collects trophies for a hockey team they call the Bruins. Sure, there is a legend who gets paid more than $130,000 a year to excite Boston fans. But, once you get off the ice, there is no Bobby Orr.

I should know. I wrote a book about Bobby Orr a while back, when there still was a real person behind the legend. But is there a real person there anymore? I've been trying to find out for a couple of years now. So have others. You'd have an easier time cracking a CIA code.

Bobby Orr, the hockey entity, is well known. The people who run the Bruins and who run Bobby Orr will tell you all about him. And there's no taking any of it away. Bobby Orr is the best hockey player in the game today. But, off the ice, Bobby Orr is the best-kept secret since the Pentagon Papers. And Daniel Ellsberg himself couldn't leak this one.

Maybe it's nobody's business. Sure, Bobby Orr is entitled

to a private life, just like the next guy. But when everybody around tries to convince you that the guy doesn't drink or curse or fool around with girls, and that the only time he takes his halo off is when he goes to bed with his stick, you have to start to wonder. You have to start to question and probe.

But how do you get past the p.r.? A journalist does not talk to Orr *just like that*. The procedure is almost as intricate as getting a seat at the Stanley Cup play-offs. First, you must contact R. Alan Eagleson of Toronto, Orr's advisor and overseer.

An attorney with William Holden overtones, Eagleson is, among other things, a high official in Canada's Progressive-Conservative Party, executive director of the National Hockey League Players' Association and, because he represents all breeds of athletes, a general Mister Ubiquitous on the sports pages of Toronto newspapers. And Orr just happens to be his 24-carat client and personal friend.

My search started many seasons ago with Eagleson. I suspected that Orr, like any other ascending luminary, thrived on publicity the way an African violet thirsts for water. So I threw down all the high cards in my hand when I phoned Eagleson. I told him the Orr interview would result in the following:

A story in *Eye* magazine, which at the time was a prestige teen-age publication of the Hearst empire.

A feature on Orr in *Maclean's,* which is regarded as the national magazine of Canada.

A story on Orr and Eagleson in my internationally syndicated hockey column.

Eagleson readily agreed, and with Madison Avenue reflexes suggested I meet Orr in early September 1968 on a day which just happened to coincide with a press conference heralding the opening of The Bobby Orr-Mike Walton Sports Camp. Since the expensive Orr-Walton project needed all the lift-off it could get, a mention of the camp in the articles would be like helium to a balloon.

Known to intimates as "Good Old Eag" or the "Eagle," the galvanic Eagleson understood the need for a lengthy interview with his prodigy. He promised that Orr would cooperate and said the young defenseman would be available directly after the press conference at Toronto's Royal York Hotel.

The conference itself was a capsulization of the banality that permeates hockey from locker room to front office. Blond and bronzed like a certified surfer, Orr shook hands with two dozen newspapermen and radio-TV types, smiled frequently and answered the precious few questions allowed with the hockey player's typically laconic reply, "Well, I don't know."

When everyone appeared satisfied, Bobby wheeled away from the crowd, looking like a pleasant enough chap who would make an enjoyable, if not stirring, subject. I approached and introduced myself. The return greeting was so warm and effusive that my first reaction was to sign up all my children for a summer at the Orr-Walton Camp. Then I pulled myself together and recalled that I had no children.

The pleasantries dispensed with at the speed of a face-off, I reminded Orr that I was there for an interview. His response had the offhand, negative thwack of an elbow he might toss at someone like Brad Park of the Rangers. "I'm on my way back to Parry Sound," said Orr. He had stopped smiling.

Parry Sound is a summer resort town situated north of Toronto on Georgian Bay. It has been immortalized as Orr's home town in much the same manner that Whittier, California has been made famous by Richard Nixon. And Bobby was headed home before we had even started. I nervously thought to myself, "Parry Sound, Parry Sound?" and then sputtered, "But, Bobby, Eagleson said. . . ."

Orr interrupted, "This is the first *I* heard about it!"

126

I had lost the face-off. Now the game was in the balance. I knew Orr wouldn't be leaving immediately because he first had to take his weekly therapy session (for a knee injury) at Maple Leaf Gardens. I had to move fast. The Eagle had to be found, and luckily I tracked him down at his Bay Street office. Eagleson was typically sympathetic and practical. "Bobby is young," he apologized. "He forgets. But don't worry, I'll work it out." I continued to worry.

Eagleson has a knack for such things and he did, in fact, work it out. Orr refused to stay in Toronto for the interview but he agreed to take me along to Parry Sound. Bobby would talk to me and I would, somehow, manage to get back to Toronto the next day.

I arranged to meet Orr at the physiotherapist's room at Maple Leaf Gardens. When we met the cloud over Orr's disposition seemed to have lifted. We walked outside to his convertible, which was illegally parked on Church Street in front of the arena's marquee. He seemed amused to find a yellow traffic ticket peeking out from under the windshield wiper blade. "That's life," he laughed, and we piled into the car and turned north for Parry Sound.

As the car rolled slowly along Yonge Street, Toronto's main drag, I was somewhat disappointed that more pedestrians didn't try to get a piece of the holy Orr. The most arresting response was the collective giggle of a trio of teen-aged girls once they had clearly established that the blond behind the wheel was Bobby Orr of the Bruins.

By this time Bobby had loosened his tie so that it hung lazily from his neck, the way commuters do on the subways at 5 P.M. He began answering questions. His replies were as much as you could expect from a twenty-year-old who had never received his high school diploma. ("My Mom keeps bugging me to go back to school," he said, "and maybe I will this fall." But he knew and I knew that he didn't mean it.) He also had the odd habit of chewing the end of his tie as he mulled over my questions.

127

At first his answers were monotonously monosyllabic, except for the occasional burst of oratory about how much he loathed former referee John Ashley. ("He skates around like a big shot.") Orr betrayed the hockey player's habitual code of silence when I asked him why the Bruins had lost the Stanley Cup play-off round to Montréal. He popped the "off-the-record" lid on our conversation and then proceeded to crisply put down Bruin coach Harry Sinden. He also confessed he loathed Rod Seiling of the Rangers, but he couldn't offer a printable reason why, so I left it at that.

With each northward mile Orr nibbled on the bottom of his tie and loosened up more and more until I actually felt that *I* could talk off-the-record to *him*. I mentioned some of the trouble I had been having with the Bruins, especially Ted Green, who had refused to talk to me after I had facetiously described him as a ragamuffin defenseman. Orr was vastly amused. "Teddy *can* get upset," said Bobby, "but don't worry, I'll patch it up for you." And he sounded like he meant it, too.

When we arrived in Parry Sound, he dropped me off at the local motel and said he'd be back in a while to take me for a cruise on Georgian Bay. An hour later he returned and drove me to the wharf where we picked up two of his hometown cronies and his father, Doug Orr, and a few six-packs of beer. Then we all buzzed off into the sunset.

Bobby sat atop the pilot's seat, steering the boat with his toes. He looked on top of the world, and when the boat docked about a half-hour later on a tiny secluded island, he proudly showed me a cabin he shared with his friends. It modestly included a sauna bath, one small light bulb, a radio so Doug could listen to baseball games and very little else.

A ritual followed. We peeled off our clothes and dove into the surprisingly warm bay. Then, out of the water and into the sauna, and then back into the bay until it was totally dark and we were exhausted. By now Bobby was playing second cousin to me; he was an amiable, unpretentious and perfect host. Within an hour we had returned to Parry Sound. Doug Orr left and the rest of us went to the local bar, where the talk invariably swung to women. I learned that there are two classes of chaseable females in Parry Sound—the summer visitors from the States, of which there are many, and the new schoolteachers arriving for the fall semester. Bobby's interest in the teachers was purely academic, since by the time they arrived he'd be away with the Bruins. After a second beer we left the empty bar and Bobby drove me back to the motel.

He arrived early the next morning and took me to breakfast at the bus station. There he indulged in some rather low-grade joking with an elderly waitress, after which we promenaded along the main drag. The proprietress of a souvenir shop completely ignored Orr while I shopped for a small gift, but the local constable traded friendly shoves with him, and his haberdasher supplied vital information about a rather comely body which had paraded past the store. Then it was back to the bus depot, a handshake and the beginning of the end of my friendship with Bobby Orr. Precisely how it deteriorated—in Orr's mind—may never be known, which is too bad because this process, more than anything, could supply some fascinating information about this young man's psyche.

When I was with them, Orr's father had shown his growing disenchantment with certain journalists, a skepticism that was to be shared by his mother and, in time, by Bobby himself. His father was peevish over allegedly faulty observations about Parry Sound weather conditions made by a *Sports Illustrated* reporter. "In that article," Doug Orr said, "he must have thought the guys in Parry Sound were boobs when he wrote that ice froze on Parry Sound in September. Why, one day in December, I drove up in the rain."

During my visit with Orr I had become so relaxed by his hospitality that I agreed to let him see the manuscript of the *Maclean's* story. That meant I first had to submit it to Bobby's attorney, Eagleson, which I did. As it turned out, the Eagle was bent on projecting Bobby to the great world beyond the NHL cocoon as a skating hunk of Ivory Soap, 99 and 44/100 percent pure. In a short time Eagleson returned the story to me, well sugar-coated, even to the point of changing such deathless Orr-atory as "what the hell" to "what the heck!"

When *Maclean's* (*Eye* was rapidly en route to the grave and no longer wanted my piece on Orr) dispatched a photographer to Orr's Boston pad, the young defenseman was found in the company of a rather luscious demoiselle and unhesitatingly posed with her. Somehow, the Eagle got wind of the photos and, no doubt appalled at the thought of Orr in the photographic company of a Boston beauty, ordered all coed scenes out of the magazine. We had no choice but to comply. As a result, Bobby appeared on the cover of *Maclean's* looking very much like the All-Canadian Boy. Score one for the Eagle.

In the meantime, *Sport* magazine commissioned me to write a lengthy article on Orr. This would require one more long interview with Bobby, so I phoned Eagleson and told him I wanted to see Orr in Boston following a Montreal-Bruins game a few days before Christmas. Always cooperative, the Eagle came through again, with no strings. But I soon found that there was a rope strangling my typewriter and it was being pulled from the direction of the Boston Garden. When I headed for the locker room after the game to set up an interview with Orr for the following day, a Bruins official barred me from the players' area.

Not wanting to start a brawl with all those Bruins around, I waited outside until Orr finally appeared. He seemed surprised and not at all happy to see me. "I can't make it tomorrow," he said. Then there was a long pause. "But Tuesday is okay," he said and he agreed to meet me at my room at Logan International Airport Motel.

Orr did show up for the interview, and he did talk. But the *intime* of Parry Sound had given way to a stiff reserve. He answered questions for an hour, and then begged off to keep a date. As the off-white turtleneck disappeared behind the closed door I had no idea that this would be one of my last friendly confrontations with Prince Valiant. Maybe I was wrong about Orr, I thought. So what if he was somewhat abrupt? After all, I had milked him for everything he had to say, from Toronto to Parry Sound to Logan Airport. My notes were copious and I returned home prepared to write endlessly about Bobby Orr. Which I did.

By sheer coincidence the *Maclean's* article appeared on the day of the 1969 NHL All-Star Game in Montreal. Orr's boyish profile was splashed on the cover and the story brought nothing but compliments from my colleagues. The clincher was a warm endorsement from Bob Haggert, Orr's close friend and business associate. "That story," said Haggert, "was the greatest!"

At the press reception that night, Orr appeared amiable. He said he hated crowds and seemed content to stand in the corner and gab with me about nothing in particular. Apparently he hadn't seen the *Maclean's* article. At least, he said nothing about it. Later, I walked over to Bruin defenseman Ted Green and held out my hand. He repeated what he had said on other occasions, "Bugger off!" He is a witty one.

A few days after I returned home, I got a long distance call from Orr. The surprisingly harsh voice hit me like the screeching of subway wheels on a sharp curve. "Teddy Green was right about you," Orr snapped. And then he went on about how I had done him in by writing in *Maclean's* that he had poured himself a beer. It was only an

131

obscure line in a long paean of praise, but he jumped me for writing it.

"I'm too *young* to be shown having a beer," he insisted. "It's against the *law*." When I explained that his friend Haggert had praised the story, he calmed down, but only momentarily. "Listen," he demanded. "I want to see that *Sport* magazine article before it goes in. Y'hear?"

I agreed, reluctantly, to send him a copy of the manuscript, confident that there could be nothing that would grate him this time. No beer. No four-letter words, except maybe "darn."

As promised, the article went out to Orr. I eagerly awaited its return, but nothing happened. Frustrated, I phoned Orr. "Yeah," he said, "I got it but haven't had a chance to look at it." I reminded him of the phenomenon called deadline, and he promised to read the piece. Another week. Nothing. A phone call. "Sorry," he said, "I must have lost it." A new copy went out in the next mail. No word. Another call. This time Orr said he had shown it to a girl friend. He hadn't got it back from her yet but said he would take care of the matter. I never did receive it, nor any further comment from Orr. The story appeared in *Sport* and was toasted by Bobby's courtiers. I almost felt good again.

Since there were no beer drinking scenes in the *Sport* profile and since Orr didn't phone to complain, I assumed he rather enjoyed the story. A short time later, I spoke with Eagleson and Haggert, and we talked rather vaguely about doing a book about Orr. That spring the Bruins and Canadiens met in another Stanley Cup play-off and interest in hockey was high along publisher's row. Peter Weed, an editor at Dodd Mead, asked me for an idea. I promised him that the Bruins would win the Stanley Cup—they didn't—and suggested a book about the team. He agreed and we planned a book to be divided in three parts—(1) the first known published history of the Bruins, (2) profiles of the leading Boston players, and (3) a profile of Orr based on my *Maclean's* and *Sport* magazine articles. It was to be called *Bobby Orr and the Big, Bad Bruins.*

We considered a book devoted solely to Orr, but at the time there was considerable question whether his seemingly delicate knee would bring about a swift end to his career. In case it did, we would still have the two sections on the club's history and the other stars. It never dawned on me that Bobby would dislike the book; it was a big plus for him, and his Bruins cronies were favorably treated. I also hoped that the Bruins management would appreciate the colorful history of Boston hockey.

I couldn't decide whether to notify Orr of the project. It was mid-summer, long before publication, so I decided to get in touch with Eagleson, who had been so helpful in the past. But before I had a chance to phone him he phoned me. He told me that Orr had heard about the book and wanted to know more about it. I explained the contents to Eagleson and said I'd write Orr about it, which I did. Orr never replied—and I never spoke with him again. He didn't return my phone calls, and when his unlisted number was changed, Eagleson made it quite clear that Bobby was not interested in talking to me.

The book was published and won this from *Saturday Review:* "This book will be a joy for any true hockey fan, particularly if he's young and lives around Boston. Good readable stuff." In spite of that, I began hearing threatening sounds from other writers about the consequences if I dared enter the Bruins' dressing room. Soon the time came when my job made it necessary for me to do just that. Derek Sanderson and I had contracted to write his autobiography. Being in the Bruins' dressing room would help me add color to the book, so I telephoned the club president, Weston Adams, Jr.

Adams ingenuously informed me that he didn't have jurisdiction over the dressing room and switched me to general manager Milt Schmidt. "Yes," said Schmidt, "you can *not* come into the room. For one thing, I don't like the things you've written about the club, and for another, the players don't want you in. Besides, I can't guarantee your safety in there."

Players? Safety?

Sanderson and I had been getting along beautifully ever since I had interviewed him and done a cover story in *Maclean's*. I had just collaborated with goalie Gerry Cheevers on a magazine piece that had put a few hundred dollars in his pocket, and Cheevers was friendly when we talked on the phone. My old enemy Green was not in Boston at the time, having been injured in a preseason brawl. That seemed to leave Orr as the man behind the embargo. But Eagleson insisted that Bobby wouldn't do a dastardly thing like that—not to me or to any sportswriter.

It was time to take stock. Perhaps I was being unfair to Orr. Maybe he was, as they say in Brooklyn, a real sweetheart. To find out, I avoided the flunkies on the hockey beat who worship Bobby's every pronoun and began asking the opinion of some of the more objective newsmen—Dan Proudfoot of the Toronto *Globe and Mail,* Leigh Montville of the Boston *Globe,* Jack Olsen of *Sports Illustrated* and Eddie Andelman of "Sports Huddle" on Boston's Radio Station WEEI.

Andelman wasted no time putting down Orr. "He's not the humble kid they're making him out to be," Eddie said. "He's more like the way people think Derek is. The public actually is confused." According to Andelman, the Bruins, as a team, will unofficially blacklist any writer or broadcaster who puts a heavy rap on Orr. Eddie speaks from experience. Not long after I quoted him in *The Sporting News* as having made a rather unkind remark about Orr, he shepherded 250 fiercely loyal Boston hockey fans to the West Coast to see the Bruins in action. Eddie later reported that many of the players were conspicuously rude to some of his charges—their own fans. He insists that the Boston players had conspired to ignore many of the "Sports Huddle" troupe.

"When we returned to Boston," said Andelman, "Eddie Johnston (the goalie and Bruins' players' rep) told me that the players had discussed my *Sporting News* quotes about Bobby on the plane and had decided that they couldn't allow that, so they were going to ignore us as punishment."

A reporter for a Boston daily confirmed Andelman's appraisal of the "strike-Orr-and-you're-out" syndrome. He cautioned against using his name because he still wanted to deal amicably with the Bruins. But a new slant on Bobby had gotten around, even as far west as Chicago.

"The beat guys are getting down on Orr," said a Chicago *Tribune* reporter. "He hides in the trainer's room after a game and doesn't say beans. And he acts like a ---- with most writers. He just plays and picks up his check and leaves."

"There are people," Orr has stated, "who say I'm not worth that much money. You get it a lot of ways. I used to have a brush haircut but I let my hair grow. Now some people bug me about getting a haircut. At the games you get a few wolves here and there. But you've got to take the good with the bad. Just about everybody has been super. I mean, there's just no easier way of making a living."

Sports Illustrated voted Bobby its 1971 "Sportsman of the Year," yet author Jack Olsen depicted Orr in a series of episodes that hardly fulfilled the Boy Scout image. For example—he drove his El Dorado out of a private parking lot, cutting off another car. He crossed a double yellow line. He gunned the car the wrong way up a one-way street and told off a maitre d'hotel in a restaurant outburst.

"Bobby was in a bad mood," said Olsen when I asked him about the incidents. "The Bruins had just lost a game. After all, he's human. He's not Jesus Christ, but he is a marvelous guy."

135

Dan Proudfoot was less generous. Writing in the Toronto *Globe* magazine, he said: "Orr only occasionally has to listen to jeers, and he doesn't take them well." But that, he added, is what you'd expect from anyone facing his pressures. "He's a victim of circumstances."

Even the commercialism is inevitable. Proudfoot spoke to a junior hockey acquaintance of Orr's who noted that a spate of Bobby Orr pizza places had opened. "How cheap sounding can he get?" the player said. "He's changed, he's out for the buck like the rest of them." The Orr pizzerias increased in number from two to seven. Eagleson staunchly defended the project. "Calling it cheap," the Eagle said, "is a matter of opinion. We believe they produce a top quality product and it brings Bobby a substantial amount of money."

At a press conference in Boston late in the summer of 1971, Orr let the world know—in general terms, of course—just how many bucks he would be making in the next few years. He was supposed to announce that he had signed his new contract. Instead, he revealed that he had signed it months before. Many observers were left with the feeling that they had been faked out. Even in Bobby's beloved Boston his image was beginning to deflate.

Eagleson explained that he had wanted to make the announcement in February 1971, but Orr preferred to delay it until after the playoffs. Then, the Bruins asked for another delay until, ultimately, the conference was held just before the opening of the 1971-72 training camp.

At WBZ, Dick Stockton delivered an elaborate put-down of the contract announcement ceremonies. "The whole thing was ridiculous," he told me later. "Here they are, having a news conference for a guy who had signed his contract months and months earlier. What's happened here is that the kid walks around with a halo surrounding him. The Bruins put him on a pedestal and cater to his wishes."

That's understandable. When Orr was signed by the Bruins as an eighteen-year-old, with the biggest buildup in the history of the National Hockey League, the Bruins were groping aimlessly in the NHL cellar. In the six seasons prior to Orr's rookie year, Boston had finished last five times and next to last once.

Within two years, Orr had won the Calder Trophy as rookie of the year, the Norris Trophy as the league's best defenseman and was named to the first All-Star team. With him, the Bruins climbed to contention and, finally, to the Stanley Cup championship.

Bruins' fans have adopted Orr as their very special baby boy, and anyone who dares attack him is regarded with a special contempt. Once, when a Detroit player was penalized two minutes for hooking him, an annoyed fan shouted, "Make that a two-and-a-half minute penalty—two minutes for hooking and an extra thirty seconds for hooking Bobby Orr!"

In a way, though, neither the Bruins nor Bobby Orr himself can be blamed for this attitude. Americans have always tended to enshrine their sports stars, and the press generally goes along with such hero worship. Joe Marshall, in his articles on Howard Cosell in *Esquire,* put it this way: "The idea of image, so unfortunately American, long ago enveloped the world of games. We learned to call the best players in sports All-American and created mythic heroes like Jack Armstrong. And so our athletes were automatically endowed with virtues that had nothing to do with their ability to throw a football or hit a baseball. . . ."

Eagleson calls Bobby a complicated person who is understood by few. "He shies away from involvement with people," the Eagle says. "He's not like you or I or anyone else I know. He's a very tough guy to figure out. Yet, when the chips are down he's there. He's the most dependable athlete I ever met. Other guys give you a front, but if you try to get them to visit a hospital for crippled children or something like that they don't show up; they're too busy. But Bobby will be there.

"As for his socializing, he likes his privacy, and, remember, his private hours are few. He's not a gregarious type, and it's obvious that he suffers from the envy of others."

Maybe so, but Bobby Orr is different not only from you and me and Alan Eagleson, but from most other sports figures as well. As the Boston *Globe's* Leigh Montville said when describing Bobby's inaccessibility during the Montreal-Boston play-offs of 1971:

"He dressed and undressed for every game in the trainer's room. His exits were quicker than if Clark Kent had discovered trouble somewhere on the far side of town."

Montville accused Orr of being less accessible than Howard Hughes and added: "The shield of shyness covers all sins and blunts all questions . . . Orr has received the best press imaginable. He hasn't said much of anything, so he hasn't said anything controversial. . . . The image has been built visually. He has become as clean as Ajax. . . . The salesmanship has been spectacular."

Of course I too have been swept along by the salesmanship. And with Bobby Orr, all sales are final. If he or anything about him ventures into the marketplace, it'll be on his terms and at his prices.

It's still the same old story, just like in his pizza parlors—cash and carry. Sometimes it's just a little hard to swallow.

For example, a photographer who went into the Bruins locker room one season to take some nice portrait pictures of Orr got an idea of what Bobby really is like.

"OK," Orr told him, "you've got two minutes."

The cameraman was miffed, but he realized that he had to do it on Orr's terms or not at all.

"Fine," he said, "but I'd like to get a better background.

Could you move over in front of the wall?"

"No," said Bobby Orr, ending the session.

I wasn't about to let Orr get off the hook. Once in a letter to both him and Eagleson, I offered to meet him one-on-one anywhere, anytime! Finally, on January 16, 1972, in an interview with Bill Kipouras, of the Boston *Herald-Traveler,* Orr said he wanted to see me. When I read this in Kipouras's article, I nearly fell off my chair. Orr's "facts" were unreal:

"I've only talked with him [Fischler] once," said Orr. "I'd like to talk to him again—you know, sit down—and get his thinking."

So what if Orr's memory had erred, this was my big chance. I phoned Steve Fredericks of Boston radio station WEEI, who is friendly with Orr. "Steve," I said, "Orr wants to talk to me. Why don't you arrange it?" He was very interested. Not long afterward, I received a telephone call. It was Fredericks calling while ON THE AIR. "I just talked to Bobby Orr," Fredericks told me and his vast radio audience. "He's willing to come on the air with you if you are."

I agreed wholeheartedly and asked Steve to name the time and place. He said he'd get back to me as soon as the 1972 Stanley Cup playoffs were over. I'm still waiting.

I called Bobby Orr's bluff, and I'll call it again. Meanwhile, you, me and the rest of the fans who want to know what Bobby Orr *really* is all about are still in the lurch. Is there really a Bobby Orr? Is the image for real? Does the Bobby Orr we think we know really live, breathe and eat Wheaties? Maybe. But we'll never know because Bobby Orr will never tell us.

X

THE DEREK SANDERSON EPISODE

Of all the players in the National Hockey League, Derek Sanderson was the last one I ever expected to collaborate with on a book, especially at the start of the 1969-70 season. The reasons were simple. My feuds with Ted Green and Bobby Orr had by now become international incidents. The Bruins had barred me from their dressing room and several of the players had made it abundantly clear that if I somehow managed to crack the security barriers outside the Bruins' lair, they would rend me limb from limb, or some similar torture befitting an irreverent hockey writer.

At one point I phoned general manager Milt Schmidt on a long-shot chance that perhaps the anti-Fischler restrictions might have been eased. After all, the Bruins were experiencing unmatched prosperity both artistically and financially. Surely this would inspire the Adams family and Green and Orr to commute my sentence. "No," Schmidt said, in a desperate but futile attempt to keep from shouting, "you can not go into our dressing room."

"But I have a legitimate working press card just like the other newspapermen, and over the years I've been in your dressing room about seventy-three times."

"I can not let you in," Schmidt said with the finality of a bank attendant closing a vault at the end of a day, "because I can not guarantee the safety of your life. The players don't want you in."

Yet, I wrote the book with Derek Sanderson during that 1969-70 season, and how I did it remains a constant amazement to me—something akin to a .220 hitter coming up with a .310 average for one season of his life. It started off as a lark. I had followed Sanderson's career ever since he had established himself as an A-number-one troublemaker playing Junior A hockey for the Niagara Falls Flyers in the Ontario Hockey Association. He won the NHL rookie-of-the-year award in 1968, and by 1968-69 had displayed a few idiosyncracies of conduct that alarmed the hockey Establishment. He also was a very good hockey player but this fact was concealed by coach Harry Sinden, who insisted on using Derek for defensive purposes while allowing Phil Esposito the luxury of scoring goals from the center ice position.

Nevertheless, my instincts told me Sanderson would be a hot item within a year, two at the very most. I sensed this because a) he loved to say things that no other hockey player dared say; b) he enjoyed fighting almost as much as he savored a good lay, and c) he was one of the few hockey players then in the stable of Boston sports attorney Bob Woolf, who never took on any athletes unless he expected they would soon be big-time if they weren't already.

Woolf also happened to be the attorney for Ted Green. I assumed that Green had told his representative about my countless sins against the Bruins and that a meeting with Sanderson was as unlikely as Derek winning the Lady Byng Trophy for good sportsmanship.

In this instance my radar was misleading. Having a tentative commitment from *Maclean's* for a profile of Sanderson, I phoned Woolf, explained who I was, what I wanted and waited for him to reply, "Thanks, but no thanks!"

141

"When do you want to do it?" Woolf replied. Stunned, I said I would be glad to interview Derek anytime it was convenient for him, in New York, Boston or Labrador if necessary. Woolf said he would check it out with Sanderson and get right back to me.

I was higher than a kite for about two minutes, or as long as it took me to realize that while Woolf had no qualms about setting up an interview—he was probably unaware of my war with half the Bruins team including Green—Sanderson would surely squash it and that would be that.

Two days passed before Woolf returned my call with the news. "Derek," he said, "would love for you to come up to Boston on Sunday and do the interview at his apartment. If it's all right with you, I'll drop over too. I'd like to meet you." I was in business! Only the last sentence of Woolf's acceptance speech turned me off. During my fifteen-year career as a newspaperman and magazine writer I invariably experienced problems when publicity men, agents or attorneys sat in on the interviews I was conducting with their clients. Why should Robert G. Woolf, Esq. be an exception? What I didn't realize at the time was that Woolf had shrewdly deduced that the more flamboyant and popular his clients, the higher the negotiating plateaus he could reach for them. My article would spread the Sanderson message. All our best interests converged.

I flew to Boston with a tape recorder that was on the verge of a nervous breakdown—my wife had miraculously repaired it moments before I was scheduled to leave—and a head filled with thoughts of doom. "Surely," I said to myself, "this is all a plot cooked up by Ted Green and Bobby Orr. They are luring me to Boston as a joke, using Woolf as the middleman."

Our interview was scheduled for 1 P. M. at Sanderson's apartment. I arrived in Boston at 11 A. M., rented a car and

142

spent the next hour practicing with my tape recorder, no doubt exploring every possible means to break the damn thing so I'd have an excuse to get out of this absurd charade.

The apartment, in an upper-middle-class section of Boston, actually belonged to Ken Harrelson, who then was playing baseball with the Cleveland Indians. Harrelson and Sanderson were both Woolf's clients and had become fast friends. In fact, Harrelson entertained a woman in the next room during much of my interview with Derek.

Sanderson was at the door seconds after I rang and welcomed me as warmly as I could expect under the circumstances. At a time when hockey players were still wearing crew cuts, he sported bell-bottomed sideburns and razor-cut hair.

He took my jacket and invited me over to the bar, insisting that he had no objections to my turning on the tape recorder. I said a brief prayer, trying to figure out just what would be the proper Hebrew prayer for making uncertain tape recorders work, and pressed the buttons. We were off!

Usually it takes days, if not weeks—if ever—to soften up a hockey player for a really solid interview. My strategy with Sanderson was to steer clear of the really outrageous questions at the beginning for fear of antagonizing him. But within a minute it became apparent that Derek was the one-in-a-million hockey player that I had waited fifteen years to interview. He would say *anything. Anything!* And it scared me.

Every one of the 500 hockey players I had interviewed previously had observed certain taboos. They were reluctant to antagonize the opposition, no doubt on the theory that some day the opposition would clop them good on the head. They did not discuss women, since every autograph-seeking kid from Penticton to Portage La Prairie believed all hockey players are virgins. And they certainly did not condemn the Establishment, especially NHL President Clarence Camp-

143

bell, because the Establishment is mean enough and strong enough to catapult any of them into a ditch-digging career if they don't watch out.

Sanderson, however, shocked me. First he said he would mount the heads of several prominent opponents, including Gordie Howe and Bobby Baun; then he crucified Clarence Campbell, calling him "a stuffed shirt"; and finally he showed me his bedroom with circular bed and ceiling-mounted television camera that enabled his friends to watch him with his lady of the night on closed-circuit TV in other rooms. It was, to say the least, awesome. And there was no end in sight to his monologue. "Give me the ten best-looking women in the city and I'll play for nothing . . . almost. . . . The square hockey world can use a change, and I'm the guy to change it. . . . I've never said a thing I'm sorry for in all my life."

Precisely at that point—only five minutes into the interview—I realized that Derek Sanderson was a book, not just a magazine article. But, first things first. I soon began to grasp his motives. Maybe he did, in fact, know how much I was despised by Ted Green, Bobby Orr and Phil Esposito. But apparently that didn't matter to Derek because there was something about Fischler that he liked. More than anything, it had to do with his philosophy on how to make it in the NHL.

"There are three things you need to make money in professional sport," he said. "One is talent. The second is points. The third is color. Bobby Orr has the talent. Esposito has the points. The only thing left for me is the color!"

Suddenly, the doorbell rang. A husky man in golf clothes and five o'clock shadow entered—it was Bob Woolf. He clasped my hand firmly—too firmly—when we were introduced and asked if I'd mind if he sat in on the interview. Of course I'd mind! With Woolf looking over my shoulder, I was certain Derek would clam up, and even if he didn't,

Woolf would censor every other quote Sanderson delivered or put bland words in his mouth for him.

"No, Bob," I said with a tight grin on my face, "by all means sit down and join us."

Instead of holding back, Derek seemed to accelerate his outrageous observations. "When Milt Schmidt saw my long sideburns at training camp," said Derek, "he was sick. He said, 'Cut those things off!' I said to him straight, 'Don't worry about how I cut my hair. How I play hockey is all you got to worry about.' "

As our conversation continued, I saw Sanderson as a hip Clint Eastwood, his dark sideburns arched above a frilly yellow shirt cut to the navel, setting off cream-colored hip-huggers. He poured a gin-and-tonic for me and a Coke for himself. "Sex and hockey—you wanna know my theory?" he went on. "Everything in moderation. If I'm going to be with a broad the night before a game, I'll take her to dinner at eight o'clock, get home at nine, ball her until midnight, then go to sleep. For me, I know I've got to have my rest, right? I plan everything I do with the game in mind."

And so it went on into the afternoon until I ran out of tape. There was absolutely nothing that Sanderson considered off-limits. He told about how he traded girl friends with Rod Gilbert and Bob Nevin, players on the supposedly hated Rangers, and he talked about how his father collected the thread from the first 100 stitches of Derek's hockey-playing career and put it in a glass jar. I left Sanderson's apartment with that rare "high" a newspaperman gets when he comes away with that once-in-a-lifetime story. I felt like a just-opened bottle of vintage Burgundy.

There was only one catch. Bob Woolf not only left Derek's apartment with me but insisted that I drop over to his house for a few minutes. He said his friend and client John Havlicek, the basketball player, was there and he'd like me to meet him. At that point I wanted to meet Havlicek about as much as I did the tax collector, but Woolf was so

145

insistent that I had to accept. I was certain that he wanted a half hour to talk me into killing the best parts of my interview.

With every passing minute on our drive to suburban Brookline, I expected Woolf to mutter, "You know, Stan, there are a few things that Derek said that I don't think belong in a magazine article . . ." But he never said it. He asked me if I had had enough time with Derek and whether I wanted to see him again and was there anything else he could do for me. It was as if my Christmas and Hanukkah presents for the next ten years had been delivered all at once. I wasn't aware of it at the time, but the meeting with Derek began what was to become a lengthy acquaintanceship between me and Bob Woolf.

Phil Sykes, my editor at *Maclean's*, could hardly believe some of the quotes I relayed to him the next day, but every one of them was right on that sweet little seven-inch reel. Sykes dispatched Horst Ehricht, one of the best photographers in Canada, to Boston, and Derek obliged by posing both in and out of bed with a bevy of beauties. That convinced me that there was no time to waste. I had to sell somebody on the idea of a Sanderson book.

I had just completed *Bobby Orr and the Big, Bad Bruins* for Dodd Mead, and my editor there, Peter Weed, listened to the Sanderson tape. An avid hockey fan, Weed was interested, but it was difficult to persuade him that a man who had scored only twenty-four goals was worth a book. Within a week, however, I got the word—yes, let's give it a try.

I immediately phoned Woolf and told him we had a deal. He told me we had *no* deal! Dave Anderson, *The New York Times* sports columnist and my predecessor on the hockey beat at the *Journal-American,* had phoned ten minutes earlier with a book proposition. Anderson, one of the best in the sports-writing business, was collaborating with Dick Schaap, who had been pumping out a series of successful sports books. Now, they wanted to do hockey and Sanderson was the man.

My white flag went up and I thanked Bob for his help. "You're still in the running," Woolf insisted. "We'll go to the best bidder, and they haven't bid yet; all they did was say they're interested."

It was August 1969 and time for a European vacation. My experience told me not to write off the Sanderson project, but my knowledge of the writing business and Schaap's available money led me to conclude that the odds were 25 to 1 against my writing Derek's book. On the flight back from Paris in September the odds climbed to 250-1 when I picked up a copy of *Newsweek* and read a feature about Schaap's book factory. Among his upcoming projects, it said, was a book about a rabbi, a basketball player—and Derek Sanderson. Damn!

Schaap and Anderson obviously were not fooling around. They supplied Derek with a tape recorder and sent him to the Bruins training camp with instructions to talk into the machine at any time and not to spare the purple prose. He didn't either. There was only one problem. At the start of the new season, Sanderson seemed to be on a daily commute between his apartment and the hospital with little time spent on Boston Garden ice in between. At one point it seemed that his career actually might be over because of an assortment of physical ailments. Suddenly the Schaap-Anderson combine lost interest in the book.

I nudged Peter Weed at Dodd Mead, and he responded with the kind of enthusiasm I needed at the time. Yes, he still wanted to do the book. By now Woolf and I had developed a regular twice-a-week telephone friendship. He promised to set a deadline with Schaap; if Dick didn't come up with a commitment, the book would go to Fischler.

Then, the turning point arrived. Late in October 1969 the November issue of *Maclean's* hit the stands. Plastered on the front cover was a brilliant color photo of Sanderson, nude

147

from the waist up. The headline shouted: *"Boston's Cocksure Derek Sanderson—Hockey's Joe Namath."*

By any standards it was a socko piece. The writing was good, the photography was excellent—especially a two-page color spread of Derek horizontal in bed with a voluptuous girl friend, both clothed—and all those juicy quotes were alive and kicking on the pages of *Maclean's*. The Bruins front office cringed as they read, "The Montreal Canadiens don't have the team, the defense, the talent or the guts" and "I don't care who he is; his face will bleed just like mine, right? That hockey stick is a great equalizer. I've cut people so often I can't remember who, or when."

Both Derek and Woolf savored the article. Woolf never changed his mind, although Sanderson, under obvious pressure from the front office, later charged that he was being unfairly portrayed as a sex symbol. Those who know him best are certain his tongue was well ensconced in his cheek.

I thought the article would cinch me the book deal, but Schaap and Anderson hadn't quit. They made a grandstand bid, offering something like $5,000—I'm not sure of the precise figure—simply to keep their hand in. Schaap sensed that Derek would be a hot item if and when his injuries disappeared, and he projected a book some time in the future.

By now Derek and Woolf could taste the book, especially Derek. "He doesn't want to wait anymore," Woolf assured me. "We're going to do the book with you." Perhaps I should have been elated, but I wasn't. The emotion was more like that experienced by the warriors at Verdun in 1917. Victory is achieved, to be sure, but the exhaustion in achieving it subdues the pleasure of triumph. Now, it was a matter of getting Derek to put a book together.

It appeared to be a simple matter. Sanderson had a lot to say; he wanted to say it; and he was an excellent story-teller, which meant that we would have plenty of rich material on his childhood—which I think is the best part of the book—and his junior hockey days in Niagara Falls. It was not a simple matter, however.

Week after week passed while contract negotiations lumbered on and my troubles with the Bruins' front office mounted. *Bobby Orr and the Big, Bad Bruins* came out and became an instant best seller for a hockey book. Orr, according to reports I heard, was furious because he wasn't receiving a share of the royalties. He had become the leader of the team and had apparently spread his anti-Fischler gospel to the rest of the team. This made it enormously difficult for me because I had planned to visit the Bruins' dressing room several times to gather material for the Sanderson book. But Schmidt, apparently with the approval of the Bruins hierarchy, still kept me out.

As far as I could determine, I was being prevented from doing my professional job simply because a sports organization disliked the content of my writing and because one or more athletes didn't like me personally. It seemed like a rudimentary case of discrimination without legal foundation, so I petitioned the National Hockey League Writers Association, of which I still was a member, and demanded that the group force the Bruins to admit me.

Obviously this would not happen overnight, if at all, so I made alternate plans for handling the book. Contracts were finally signed in February, and we were ready to go. To my surprise Derek appeared genuinely enthused about the project despite the anti-Fischler flak generated by the Bruins.

"Y'know," he told me one day, "Bobby (Orr) is really pissed off at you about that book you did."

I acknowledged that I was aware of Orr's position and was about to ask Derek how he felt about it, but he had the answer before I could open my mouth. "He's getting too

149

excited over the whole thing." He left it at that. It was Orr's problem, and it wasn't going to affect his relationship with me.

Yet, somehow we never managed to get the project into orbit. The Bruins were in the home stretch of a neck-and-neck race for first place with Chicago and Sanderson couldn't—or wouldn't—be pinned down for a final conference to outline the book. On the plus side were the gallons of ink Sanderson began accumulating in newspapers and magazines across the continent. By late in the winter of 1970 his health had become perfect again and his charisma kept climbing to a point where he was as popular as Orr in Boston and considerably more popular than teammate Phil Esposito, although Phil was outscoring him by a ratio of better than two-to-one. Esposito, incidentally, never could understand Sanderson's popularity, and it annoyed him greatly.

Sanderson's appeal reached its crest early in April 1970, which coincided with the high point of our friendship. I phoned Derek frequently, and he began to confide in me for the first time. He was invited to appear on both the Merv Griffin and Johnny Carson shows—a feat never claimed by Esposito—and was profiled by *The New York Times* as the "Man In The News" after he ignited a massive brawl with several Rangers at Madison Square Garden during the first round of the Stanley Cup playoffs.

"Let's get going on the book," Sanderson said encouragingly after taping the Griffin show. "I'm all excited about it." Woolf confirmed that Derek, in fact, was champing at the editorial bit, and so we made plans. After the playoff against the Rangers, I would visit Boston several times to tape Derek's life story and get his feelings about the current hockey scene and season. The book's prospects got a boost when Boston defeated New York in six playoff games, thus qualifying for the semi-final round against the Chicago Black Hawks. The longer the Bruins remained a contender for the Stanley Cup, the better the book's saleability the next fall.

Then, however, the roof fell in. I was ready to take the train to Boston and phoned Woolf to arrange my first taping session with Sanderson. Woolf's voice had that unmistakeable signal of imminent doom when he answered the phone.

"I'm afraid," he said, "that Derek does not want to do the book with you anymore."

I was standing in the kitchen at the time and, fortunately, found a chair on which to collapse as the attorney spelled out the awful news. "Apparently his teammates have put some pressure on him and possibly the front office, too."

I later learned that the Bruins management not only had advised him to drop me but graciously recommended some "approved" authors to him. I couldn't blame them. Imagine how embarrassing it would look to the Boston management if arch-foe Fischler produced two best-selling books about the Bruins in two consecutive seasons.

"What," I asked Woolf, "are we going to do about this?"

I expected that Sanderson's position was irrevocable, and that Woolf, who had many clients and projects more pressing than Sanderson and the book, would thank me for my efforts and wish me the best of luck on future books, but not the one on Derek. It was then that I realized that I had underestimated Woolf. He was not only a contact and a friend. He was a very good friend. He said he was going to do everything in his power to save our contract.

It would not be easy, however. The Bruins now had begun the semi-final round against the Black Hawks in Chicago and its management had conveniently delivered the team to a hideout outside the city. In the meantime, I spent the week alternately cursing the fates and wondering whether I wouldn't have been better off in the long run playing "house man" to the NHL. A brutal six days elapsed punctuated only by one encouraging call from Woolf.

151

"Derek has signed a contract to do the book," he pointed out. "He *has* an obligation." I marveled at Woolf's integrity.

On the morning after Boston had swept Chicago out of the playoffs in four straight games Woolf called. "Derek is here in my office," he said. "He is prepared to do the book with you. Why don't you come up today and start tonight?" He then put Derek on the phone. It was not the same Sanderson I had known before he had decided to quit the project. His manner was conspicuously aloof and abrupt, but we did make an appointment to meet that night.

The Penn Central train from New York to Boston has many advantages, especially if you're not in a hurry. I carefully planned my questions, tested my *new* casette tape recorder and vowed that if nothing else I must extend my normally limited Hungarian-rooted patience to record-breaking limits. Sanderson, I expected, was going to break my balls before our interviews were over—or at least make a hell of a try at it. This time I was right.

Woolf met me at South Station in Boston and tried to prepare me for my first encounter with Sanderson. The attorney took a realistically vague position. He said that Derek was at a friend's apartment and wasn't sure just when he would sit down and begin the taping. Already I was furious—but quietly furious since I realized that Woolf was humoring Sanderson to make him as reasonable, if not friendly, with me as possible. We drove to the apartment. I was tight as a drum, trying to anticipate Sanderson's reaction. "Stay cool!" I repeated over and over again until the words were meaningless. I hoped for the best but expected the worst. Derek, I figured, would open with an insulting remark and take off from there on his reasons for wanting out of the book. I was wrong, but as things developed his attitude was no more generous.

He was sitting in the middle of a bedroom with Ken Harrelson and Jimmy McDonough, another close friend,

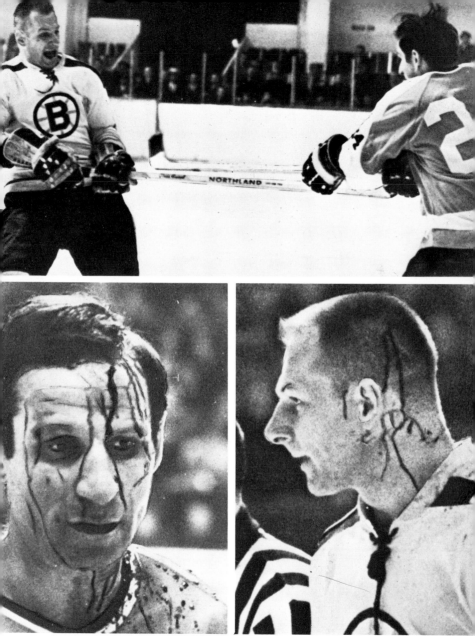

This 1968 stickfight between Eddie Shack of the Bruins and Larry Zeidel (24) of the brand-new Philadelphia Flyers really upset the hockey world. Zeidel, an old pro making his NHL comeback, was the only Jew in the league. Amid cries of anti-Semitism, photos of the bloodied Zeidel and Shack (left and right) were widely published. Eventually Zeidel led Philadelphia to a first-place finish. *(Blaise Edwards)*

A former NHL goalie, Emile "The Cat" Francis, as general manager of the Rangers, built them into Cup contenders and frequently handled the club's coaching chores behind the bench. *(Dan Baliotti)*

Sometimes attacked as a goalie who fails in the clutch, Ed Giacomin of the Rangers—here stopping a puck with his knee—has been consistently good over the past decade. *(Vincent P. Claps)*

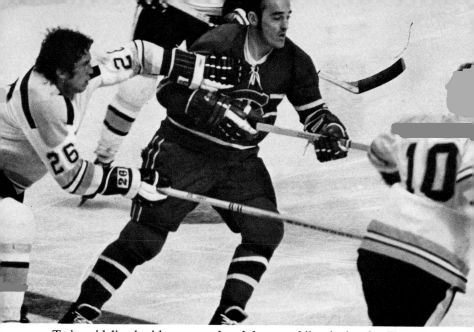

Twice sidelined with nervous breakdowns while playing for Toronto, Frank Mahovlich recovered and starred again for Detroit and, most recently, Montreal. Here he's shown among a gang of Bruins. *(Dan Baliotti)*

Stan Mikita of the Chicago Black Hawks, regarded as one of the more outspoken hockey players, is one of the best little men in the NHL. *(Dan Baliotti)*

The famous Derek Sanderson is best known for his defensive abilities, but he frequently bisects the enemy's defense for a shot; right, the foe is the Rangers. Below, Sanderson is performing one of his famous badboy stunts: after being put in the box in a 1970 Flyers game, he clambered into the stands to get a heckling fan, his teammates in hot pursuit. Below right is a much cooler—and richer—Sanderson. He'd recently accepted $1 million for letting the WHA's Philadelphia Blazers tear up their $2.5 million contract with him. He's meeting with his attorney Bob Woolf, right, and Bruins manager Harry Sinden, left, to discuss returning to the Bruins—which he later did. *(Mel DiGiacomo, UPI, UPI)*

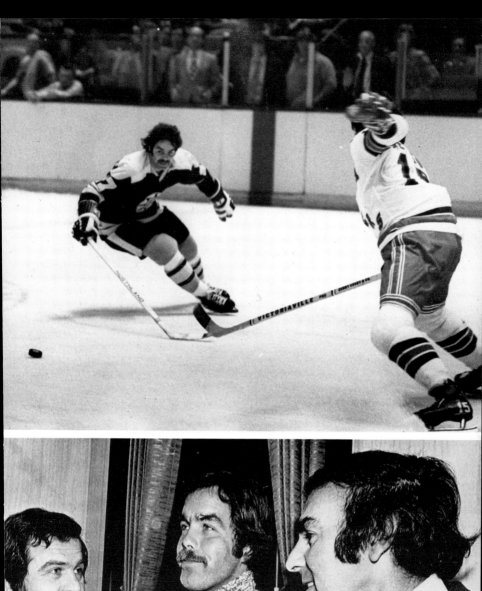

Left, Guy Lafleur, shooting the puck past New York Islanders defenseman Gerry Hart, is one of the new-breed members of the Flying Frenchmen—the Montreal Canadiens. *(Dan Baliotti)*

Bottom left, a view from the net: Henri Richard of the Canadiens zeroes in on Chicago Black Hawks goalie Tony Esposito. *(Dan Baliotti)*

Below, the man on his back happens to be none other than, who attempted to teach Ed Giacomin how to play goal. Rangers right wing Rod Gilbert, shooting the puck past me, proves I still have plenty to learn.

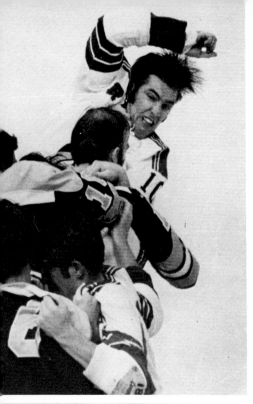

Boston and New York have never been too friendly, as is expressed in this free-for-all. Bill Fairbairn (10) of the Rangers heads the line of battling players, top, as he flails at Bruin Wayne Carleton. Bottom, the top of linesman Pat Shetler's head is outlined by the stripes of his shirt, as he's caught in the tangle of players, trying to separate them. *(UPI)*

watching a West Division Stanley Cup playoff game on television. He barely took his eyes off the set as Woolf and I entered. The "hello" he grunted was the kind you might expect him to deliver to a busboy who happened to ask him for an autograph when the maitre d' wasn't looking. His eyes immediately returned to the screen. During breaks in the game action Sanderson would occasionally turn to Harrelson or McDonough and make an observation. I rapidly developed the feeling that I might as well have been in Somaliland as far as Derek was concerned.

At last the game was over, and I hoped Derek would finally sit down with me and start talking. "Let's go eat," he said, "I'm dying of hunger." I looked at Woolf and Woolf looked at me. Docilely we followed the entourage to an exotic Polynesian restaurant. With a few drinks under my belt, I began to feel less uncomfortable. Harrelson was a big help, telling funny baseball stories and luring me into the conversation. But the hour was late, and I began to believe that Sanderson had forgotten about the taping session.

Nevertheless, I remained determined not to antagonize this spoiled child. He appeared to be seeking some way to break my spirit. Like my third base coach used to shout, "Wait him out!" so I waited, and waited.

Dinner was over at 1 A. M. "Let's go tape," said Derek with about ten degrees more warmth in his voice. "I feel like talkin'."

With Woolf as the chaperone, we drove to Derek's new apartment. It was a split-level, with beamed ceilings that gave a sort of Spanish air to the place (even the kitchen was beamed). There was a sunken living room with a wall-to-wall lime-green shag rug. In front of a cork wall there was a six-stool bar; another wall was entirely mirrored. Up the stairs was the bedroom with an eight-foot circular bed and an ankle-deep, wall-to-wall white rug. One wall was mirrored.

Stacks of mail made little mountains on the bar. They

153

were fan letters—many from women propositioning him, often with photographic enclosures—and an occasional business letter. He glanced at a couple of letters and disdainfully dropped them back on the heap.

The taping began stiffly, but it soon became clear that Derek really did want to do the book. He adopted a professional attitude, almost as if he were playing a game that he wanted to win, no matter how ornery the opposition. Within ten minutes he had moved into second gear, and before an hour had elapsed I realized that *I've Got to Be Me,* the title Derek had selected, would be the best hockey book on the market.

I never got the feeling that Derek *really* liked me, but I knew he had quickly grown to respect my hockey knowledge. He talked until his second pack of cigarettes had been chain-smoked and then called it a night—or morning. When Woolf and I departed we noticed two girls lurking across the street. "All they want is just a glimpse at Derek," Woolf said. "This kind of thing happens all the time."

Exhausted, I fell into the car, hoping that I could obtain three more sessions like the first. If so, the book would be finished in time and would be a winner. Woolf set up two appointments, one each for me and my wife, also a freelance writer, since Derek insisted that at least one interview be by a woman. "I work better with them," he said.

Our second session was the sanest of them all. Woolf and I had a Chinese dinner at 8 P.M. and drove to Derek's at 10. His companion was a thoroughly luscious young woman from Pittsburgh who uttered at most nine different words all evening. By coincidence, Sanderson had just ordered an elaborate Chinese dinner and insisted that I have some. I satisfied myself with some tea and butterfly shrimp and almost felt as if Derek had become a friend.

In a way I felt sorry for him. He obviously was a superior intellect who preferred to use a dead-end-kid facade. He was a masterful storyteller with an excellent grasp of history,

154

modern and ancient, as well as world affairs. I got the impression he could hold his own with any group of eggheads and probably out-debate them all. But this facet of Sanderson emerged only in the quiet of the living room where we talked for four hours, or until the last of the forty cigarettes was crushed in the ashtray.

Now I was beginning to worry. I'd really gotten to like the guy, and that could be dangerous. Fortunately, Derek managed to cure me of that during our last session.

While all this was going on the Bruins were in the process of wiping St. Louis out of the playoffs in four straight games. The Stanley Cup victory—Boston's first since 1941—would be the ideal closing chapter for the book. Woolf invited me up to Boston the day after the celebration and arranged an interview with Derek at the Sanderson compound. I had a solemn promise that Derek would be there no later than 4 P. M. I phoned at 4, only to learn from Miss Pittsburgh that Derek had said he would be back at 5.

It was 10:10 when he finally checked in. Not only didn't he apologize either to me or his girl friend, but he acted as if he had arrived precisely on time. No matter. The interview was good and would be completed two days later after a plane trip to New York, where Derek was to tape a *Tonight Show* with Johnny Carson.

When I returned to Woolf's house from Derek's apartment, the attorney told me he was sitting on a hot story. His client, Harry Sinden, coach of the Bruins, was about to resign only three days after the Stanley Cup victory. It was a matter of money. Sinden was furious with the condescending attitude the Boston front office had taken toward him. He had received a very lucrative offer to take an administrative job with a modular home company in Rochester, New York, and, wonder of wonders, he *was* going to take it. That is, unless Woolf could head him off at the pass.

As I sat in the attorney's study after midnight, he phoned Sinden in a final attempt to avert what would be the most embarrassing hockey episode in the Bruins' long and rich history. Sinden had made it clear that there was nothing Bruins' management could do to change his mind. "The question," said Woolf, "is whether you want to spring the announcement on the front office without giving them warning or whether you want to give them the courtesy of a final, personal good-bye."

Sinden agreed that he would visit his bosses the following morning and hold an official press conference a day later. "Maybe," Woolf told me after hanging up, "the Bruins will come through with enough money to change his mind." They didn't. Immediately after leaving the Bruins offices, Sinden returned to his suite in the Hotel Madison, next door, and met with his pal, Will McDonough of the Boston *Globe.* "They [the Bruins]," McDonough later told me Sinden said, "are a bunch of cheap bastards!"

Since I was in Boston, I decided to cover the Sinden farewell press conference for the Toronto *Star* and *The Sporting News* and also attempt to defy the Bruins ban against Fischler. It was easy. The press conference was organized by Sinden and his new employers, Stirling Homex Company, as well as Woolf. All the Bruins front office people could do was glower as I took my seat in the front row. I daresay I experienced a goose-pimply feeling of pleasure as I fired away the questions at Sinden while Milt Schmidt and cronies looked on helplessly unable to invoke their embargo.

I filed my story, met Woolf and then headed for Logan Airport, where Derek was to meet us for the flight to New York. The attorney, his wife, Ann, and I waited at the gate as the clock ticked away the remaining minutes before departure. "Do you think he'll make it?" I asked Woolf.

"If he doesn't," Bob replied, "Johnny Carson will be very unhappy."

Approximately thirty seconds before the gates were to close, Derek nonchalantly strode into view. He seemed as oblivious of his tardiness as he was the night he showed up six hours late for his taping session with me. We sat next to each other on the plane. He was—and is—genuinely afraid of flying, so it was futile to do any interviewing during the flight. We concluded the taping during the limousine ride to Rockefeller Center. For reasons best known to him, Derek had become sullen and almost mute. I had to pull the answers out of his mouth, but, thanks to a classic Manhattan traffic jam, I was able to get enough of them to complete the book.

I sat in during the TV taping, pleased to see that Carson was having as much trouble with Derek as I had had during the limousine ride. When the show was over I bade Sanderson good-bye, certain that this would be one of the last times we would see each other. I could not take much more of his contemptuous behavior, book or no book, and I'm sure that he had grown tired of my bearded face.

The book was published in November 1970, and, except for the expected raps from the anti-Fischler corps of hockey writers, it was warmly received and sold exceptionally well. Dodd Mead had hoped that Derek would help in the promotion of the book but he really couldn't be bothered.

As it turned out I had two more meetings with Derek. During the 1970-71 season he emceed his own "talk" show on a Boston television station. Bob Woolf persuaded the producer to invite my wife and me on the program. As an interviewer, Derek was at the top of his game. He fired some interesting questions at us about the problems of a husband-and-wife hockey-writing team. Then, he addressed himself to my problems with the Bruins and especially Bobby Orr. His questions were tough, but my answers were tougher than any he expected.

My last confrontation with Sanderson took place a few weeks later while I was in Boston for another book promotion. Woolf and I stopped off at Derek's apartment along with a photographer from *Time* magazine, who was doing a photo feature on chicly dressed athletes. He wanted Derek to pose outside the apartment for about twenty minutes. At his grumpy best, Sanderson refused. He seemed to be putting on a show for himself and Ken Harrelson, who was there at the time. The photographer, a free-lancer, was getting a taste of Sanderson at his worst. "Come over to the TV studio," Derek finally conceded, "and we'll shoot over there."

Woolf, who was sensitive to the photographer's problems, tried his best to comfort and stall the young man. When we got to the studio Derek discovered that he would be delayed at least an hour before his show could be taped.

For me, Sanderson vs. the photographer had become a spectator sport. I watched it with the same fascination as the survivor of a fight with Muhammad Ali would watch another pug get his brains beaten out by the former champ. Every ten minutes or so the photographer approached Sanderson and suggested that they do some shooting, and each time Derek would beg off with some excuse or another. "We'll do it when the show is over," Derek finally insisted.

The television show was taped, but I can't to this day remember a thing about it. I kept wondering about that emasculated photographer and just how Derek would treat him after the show had ended.

I walked ahead of Derek and met Woolf at the door. "Where's the photographer?" I asked.

"He left," said Woolf, "he couldn't take it any more."

Neither could I. And that's why I never bothered with Derek Sanderson again.

XI

ME AND BRAD PARK
AGAINST
THE RANGERS

If it is possible for a writer to "discover" a super star, then I go down in history, along with Carl Martin of the Hudson (New Jersey) *Dispatch,* as the co-discoverer of defenseman Brad Park of the New York Rangers. This is the way it happened.

In September 1968, I was assigned to cover the Rangers training camp in Kitchener, Ontario by the *Suffolk Sun,* the Cowles-owned Long Island daily which has since gone under. My arrival at camp immediately caused a stir because I had grown a beard and nobody, but *nobody,* in hockey wore a beard.

The beard immediately dropped me a couple of points in the eyes of several of the more conservative players, and I was viewed with a distillation of alarm and wariness. Of course, I was somewhat disturbed by the reaction, but I had prepared myself for it and was not surprised when the needles began flying in my direction.

Since the humor delivered by hockey players usually ranges from the *Alley Oop* level to bad *It Pays to Be Ignorant,* none of the wisecracks are worth repeating. I might add the writing corps also was somewhat disturbed by

159

my beard, and, naturally, no-sideburns general manager Emile Francis took an automatic dim view of my hirsute condition.

The first days of camp are virtually meaningless to a journalist. A large number of minor leaguers go through the motions trying to crack the Rangers lineup, which, at that time, was practically set. Francis had Ed Giacomin in goal, and that was plenty as far as that position was concerned. On defense were such veterans as Harry Howell, Jim Neilson, Arnie Brown and Rod Seiling. Theoretically, there would be what hockey writers like to describe as a "battle" for the fifth defense position. Actually, we all knew that there would be no battle at all. The Rangers had been grooming a tall, handsome young defenseman named Al Hamilton for three years, and it was believed that Hamilton now was ready for the big time.

At six-feet-two and 195 pounds and with three years of pro hockey under his belt, including two stints with the Rangers, Hamilton was in the "can't miss" category. Francis did throw a few other defensemen into the pot, but they were there merely to round out the roster before the first cuts were made.

For the first couple of days of training camp, the workouts consist mainly of end-to-end skating exercises to get the legs back into shape. There are few more boring moments for a hockey writer, so, on the second day of camp when the skating practice was taking place, Carl Martin and I took a walk around the Kitchener Memorial rink. As we approached one corner we noticed a man, a woman, a little girl and a young man of high school age sitting together watching the workout. For some inexplicable reason—probably simply to make conversation and break up the monotony—we stopped and sat down next to them. After an exchange of hellos, I asked them why they were so fascinated by the skating exercises.

"Well, for one thing," said the husky, gray-haired man, "my son is trying out for the Rangers."

"Really," said Martin, "which one is he?"

"He is sitting right next to you. This is Brad Park, my son. I'm Bob Park. This is my wife and daughter."

Brad was wearing a light blue sweater and had the choir boy look of someone who had auditioned for job of Rangers stick boy and failed. There was nothing in his appearance that suggested a professional hockey player. And, of course, we had never heard of him so there was only one thing to do: humor Bob Park and his son Brad. We talked about his background and learned that he had played for the Toronto Marlboros, a strong Junior club in the Ontario Hockey Association, and that he had been rejected by the Toronto Maple Leafs organization. In a matter of minutes what began as a cursory conversation began to get more and more serious. If nothing else, Martin and Fischler realized that Park and Park were deadly certain that Brad would make the team.

"How is that possible?" I asked.

"Look," said Brad, "there are five spots available, right? Well, I think I'm good enough to make one of those five. I'm going to shoot for first or second. If I don't get that high, then I'll surely be picked for the third, fourth or fifth. And as for Al Hamilton, I think I'm a better defenseman than he is; but we'll just wait and see."

By now, Martin and I were beginning to believe these people. We told them we'd be around for the next week or so and keep tabs on Brad. Then we said good-bye and walked to the arena parking lot. "You don't believe that guy do you, Carl?" I asked.

"Of course not."

"Good, because I was beginning to wonder whether they were conning you, too."

Park was one of two junior graduates Francis had placed

on the varsity defense before making his cuts. The other was Mike Robitaille, who had starred for the Kitchener Rangers junior team. Except for their faces, Robitaille and Park were almost doubles. They both were built like fireplugs, both could skate well and shoot the puck like a bullet. They would do well on the farm.

After a week had passed, Martin and I realized that Brad Park had no intentions of playing in the minors. What's more, some of his teammates were beginning to believe that, too. Brad obviously was playing better hockey than Hamilton and Robitaille, and veterans such as Howell began touting the kid. Still, nobody believed that Francis would chuck Hamilton. The feeling was that Al was having a slow start and would come around during the two exhibition games the Rangers had scheduled at Madison Square Garden.

At best, Park was an 80-to-1 shot to make the Rangers —until the first exhibition game in New York. Hamilton made one mistake after another while Park looked like a seasoned pro. The pattern was repeated in the second exhibition game, leaving Francis no choice but to keep Park on the varsity at least until the end of the exhibition run. Which is precisely what he did. But the unwritten commitment to Hamilton had to be fulfilled and it was. Park and another promising rookie, Walt Tkaczuk, were dispatched to Buffalo of the American League. Both played splendidly, while Hamilton betrayed the failings of a mediocre defenseman. After allowing Park seventeen games in the minors, Francis brought him back to Broadway, and Brad never touched a minor league uniform again.

Brad's leap to stardom was not without its detours. The Ranger coach at the time was Bernard "Boom Boom" Geoffrion, an excitable former member of the Montreal Canadiens. The Boomer, as he was known, preferred more experienced players to rookies such as Park and Tkaczuk and frequently forced Brad to vegetate on the bench.

Fortunately for Park, Geoffrion took a leave in mid-season and Francis took over the coach's duties in addition to his manager's role. Park began seeing more and more ice. His game improved and by season's end it became apparent that he would be the new Ranger ace.

In the meantime, I remained as close to Park as I could. While other reporters surrounded the so-called "star of the night," I made a point of heading straight for Brad's corner in the most distant sector of the dressing room. He was a pleasure to interview, always supplying a fresh line, never closed-mouthed like most of his teammates and invariably pleasant, no matter what had befallen him during the game.

When Brad returned for his second season in 1969-70—his first full year with the club—he progressed so rapidly he was voted to the first All-Star Team, along with Bobby Orr. Almost overnight he became the second best defenseman in all hockey, and I, by sheer luck, had become his Boswell. I wrote articles on Park for *The Sporting News, Sport, Jock* and anyone else who was interested. I had also become friendly with his parents and phoned them from time to time for information.

It didn't take very long for me to realize how strong an influence Bob Park had on his son. Bob had coached Brad almost from the time he could walk and considered himself very wise in the nuances of hockey, amateur and pro. When Bob Park spoke, I listened, and usually learned.

Meanwhile, my relationship with the Rangers management had been progressively deteriorating, although I still could get a private interview with Francis just by dialing a telephone. Francis, I later learned, was rather peeved at my wife, Shirley. Shirley, whom I married in 1968, is a freelance writer and broadcaster and occasionally does pieces on the pro hockey scene. She had been working on a story about Terry Sawchuk-Ron Stewart and her digging griped Emile; especially her interview with the goalie in Long Beach Hospital a few weeks before he died. But he

163

apparently decided to let the matter drop, incendiary as it was to the Rangers front office.

In my "heart-to-heart" discussions with Francis—all off-the-record—I felt no compunction about mentioning some of my more colorful book subjects. The Derek Sanderson book was in the works for the 1970-71 season, and I was looking for new subjects. Why not Brad Park? I had considered Brad Park, but rejected the idea for two reasons. I didn't think he'd supply enough meat the way Sanderson did, and I knew that books about New York hockey players had never done very well because there are too many diversions in New York to enable hockey to reach the level of importance shared by basketball, football and baseball.

On the other hand, my association with Sanderson had endeared me more and more to Park. It wasn't simply that Sanderson was a Class A pain; it was also that Park was so congenial and refreshing. One evening, toward the end of my Sanderson project, I visited the Rangers dressing room and asked Park whether he'd be interested in doing a book with me. He seemed delighted by the idea, which, I'm sure, was the first such offer made to him. I still was uncertain about the future of such a book but decided to query Peter Weed, who had been my editor at Dodd Mead on the Orr and Sanderson books. I had a good lever with Weed. He liked the Rangers and especially liked Park. He said he was interested.

The second time I discussed the matter with Park I was about ten times more serious than the first. He again said it was fine with him, so I contacted Weed and suggested that the three of us get together and either launch or kill the project. The meeting was arranged in April 1970, just after the Rangers had been eliminated from the playoffs. Brad and his wife-to-be were to meet Shirley, myself and Weed at a restaurant near Madison Square Garden called The Steer Palace. I'm not sure what time was arranged, but Weed,

Shirley and I sat around for what seemed like an abnormally long time and then concluded that Park didn't want to do the book after all. We were drowning our sorrows with another round of drinks when Brad and his fiancée strode in armed with apologies.

To our surprise, Brad seemed more excited about doing the book than either Weed or I was, and we had no trouble arranging its format. It would be a diary style with Brad using a cassette tape-recorder and dictating his thoughts whenever he had something on his mind.

The publisher hoped, of course, to find an angle that would make the book exciting and salable. Weed and I privately agreed that the best thing that could happen to the Park book would be the Rangers' winning the Stanley Cup. We hadn't bargained on two things—Park's determination to fight for a big Ranger contract and his willingness to speak out on *certain* explosive subjects.

About a month after our meeting the book contracts were drawn up and Brad, his fiancée Gerry, Shirley and I celebrated by having a dinner at the Homestead Steak House in Manhattan and then taking a ride on the Staten Island ferry. This was my first intimate look at Brad away from the rink and away from the business table and, I must confess, I was somewhat disappointed. For the first time I noticed that he still was a kid, and a rather unsophisticated one at that. While we were crossing New York harbor, he told a joke that a) wasn't very funny and b) had a Jew as its victim. Actually, it was a harmless attempt to get a laugh, but under the circumstances it was in poor taste. Nothing more was said about it, but I knew then and there that this was not a fellow with whom I'd be close friends.

I had learned from the Sanderson experience that one need not be a "close friend" to write a good book. We signed the contracts early that summer and arranged to stay in touch. About two weeks before Shirley and I departed for our vacation, I was stunned to learn that Brad had asked Pro Sports Inc., a New York agency that represents athletes, to handle his contract talks with Francis.

It came as a surprise because Park had been expected to line up with either Alan Eagleson or Bob Woolf. Brad explained that he liked the fellows associated with Pro Sports Inc., had discussed the matter with his father and wanted a New York firm to handle him, not some out-of-towner. In our discussions Brad's tone was surprisingly serious. I got the feeling that he was going to ask a high price and hold out to the death if Francis gave him trouble.

I was pleased that Pro Sports got the Park account. I had been friendly with Marty Blackman, Steve Arnold and Paul Marcus, the trio behind the firm, and knew that they would be an excellent source for stories about the negotiations. Late in July 1970 Blackman informed me that his firm also would be handling Vic Hadfield, Jean Ratelle and Walt Tkaczuk of the Rangers in addition to Park. This was a mighty combination to wield against Francis. I had my first big story of the summer.

The fireworks were about to begin. Two things mattered now: whether Park would be diligent about his taping and, just as important,whether he would let his punches fly free. When I returned from vacation and checked the first cassette, I knew the answer was positive on both counts. Judging by the first tape, the book would be dynamite.

Park was engaged in a bitter battle with Francis over his new contract. Emile did not like Pro Sports, Inc. He banned Blackman and Arnold from attending workouts and accused Park, Hadfield, Tkaczuk and Ratelle of trying to "sandbag" him. In the middle of training camp, Francis suspended Park and great resentment developed between player and coach—which was just fine for the book because Park was not mincing any words. Brad said Francis had made a "stupid move" when he barred Blackman and Arnold. He lashed out at Francis' psychological warfare—at one point

166

in the battle Francis had gone so far as to confiscate the four players' skates.

"What makes it so incomprehensible," said Park, "is the fact that everybody knows that in the end I'll get more money to play hockey for New York. The only question is how much, and I figure it's a waste of time for Francis to go through all the nonsense, which isn't helping him, not helping me and not helping the team. It's all a big game and a silly one at that, and sitting around doing nothing drives me nuts.

"Come to think of it, though, that's exactly what Francis may be trying to do—drive me nuts—on the assumption that the pressure will soon get the best of me and I'll give in and sign for something approximating their terms. But I'm wise to that. I simply keep busy and take my mind off negotiations."

The animosity between Francis and Park kept growing and the tapes kept getting hotter and hotter. "As the bickering went on," said Park, "I had the urge to get up and do something irrational, like belt Francis in the mouth, but I didn't."

Ratelle and Hadfield signed just before the season's opener, but Park and Tkzczuk stunned Francis and the rest of the Ranger front office by continuing to hold out. By now Francis was furious over the coverage being given the holdout and was particularly piqued by me and Gerald Eskenazi of *The New York Times,* the only other regular hockey writer who challenged Francis by siding with the players throughout the negotiations. The Rangers manager was also annoyed that Eskenazi and I were close with Blackman and Arnold. We got the correct salary figures and printed them, which in itself was unheard of in New York hockey reportage.

Park and Tkaczuk eventually did sign (they missed the first two games of the season)—and Francis held his usual press conference after the first game they played. In what I felt was a rather desperate attempt to punish Eskenazi and me for having jumped the gun, he dropped some hints that Park and Tkaczuk could have done without Pro Sports Inc.

Park and I emerged from the imbroglio as friendly as ever. We set up monthly taping sessions at his apartment. I would bring along a series of questions from which we would improvise. Brad was not as eloquent nor as harshly colorful as Sanderson; but he made up for that with dependability, and he *was* controversial, especially when it came to discussions of the Bruins. Brad spared no barbs, especially when it came to analyzing Phil Esposito who had been the NHL's leading scorer and generally regarded as a Holy-Blessed-Be-He among hockey fans.

"He (Esposito) is an extraordinary stickhandler and a superb shooter," said Park, "but he doesn't have any guts. He's carried in that department by the animals on the Boston team. Esposito runs at people from behind."

That wasn't all: "A lot of people don't realize it," Brad said, "but Esposito gets annoyed—more than the average player—when he's taken out of a play. Maybe he thinks he's too good to be touched . . . ."

Park called the Bruins "bush" and accused Bobby Orr of throwing "cheap shots." In an insightful moment, he compared the Boston hockey club to a schoolyard bully. "Push the little guy around as long as the little guy won't fight back. But when the little guy fights back, the bully doesn't know what to do. That happens to the Bruins." Only one thing worried me. Francis knew that Park was writing a book with me. (In fact, Brad took notes on Francis' behavior during one of their private meetings.) Brad had promised Francis a chance to read the manuscript before it went to press. Although Francis had no *legal* right to interrupt progress or censor the finished manuscript, at any point he could put the well-known managerial pressure on Park. The thought that he might do this in some fit of pique along the way really bothered me after my experiences with Orr and Sanderson.

Through the first half of the season, Park showed no signs of wavering, despite harassment from teammates. He faithfully carried his tape recorder on road trips and dictated his reactions to the scene around him. He was reluctant to tell all only when it came to his fellow Rangers. He confided to me that he disliked a few players, and put down some others, but he insisted that these bits be omitted from the book.

I had no choice. Much as I might have wanted to use them, Brad did have the final editorial say and could delete any passage he desired. Otherwise, Brad had been as cooperative as I could have hoped.

We prepared for the home stretch. I thought it would be prudent if I stayed as far in the background as possible and didn't badger Brad about the work to be done. As a result, I spent less and less time in the dressing room on the theory that Park would become too self-conscious and get needled so much by his teammates he might decide to chuck the whole thing.

Complicating matters was the continuing deterioration in Francis' relationship with me and Gerry Eskenazi of the *Times*. This time the *cause célèbre* was Eskenazi's book about the Rangers, *A Year on Ice,* which had come out during the season. It was a chronicle of the previous year's play and was a pretty entertaining book.

What enraged Francis was the section in which Eskenazi described prostitutes at the Rangers' motel in Kitchener near the team's training site, and one specific scene in which a woman dashed out of a player's room, partially clothed, and screaming. Instead of ignoring the book and that segment, Francis attempted to embarrass Eskenazi in front of the entire Rangers team and, as a result, to induce the players *not* to talk to the *Times'* man.

In a meeting with Francis at his Madison Square Garden office, I asked him about the episode. "Imagine that Eskenazi," he indignantly shouted. "Here's a guy who came into hockey without knowing a damn thing about the sport, and I spent time teaching him things—took him under my wing—and then he writes crap like that. Can you imagine what *that* did for the team!"

We only briefly discussed the Park book and Francis made it clear that he wanted to see the manuscript. Since Brad already had agreed to show it to him, I had no choice but to agree. It was one of the last civil discussions we had.

The Rangers, as usual, relinquished their hold on first place and entered the season's homestretch behind Boston. Francis became more and more anxious, invoking bans here and there to keep his players' minds "on hockey." I began wondering what effect this would have on Park and got my answer when Brad injured his knee and was sidelined for the critical weeks of March. My hope was that Brad could relax in the grandstands, come up with a ton of new insights and give us a socko second half of the book. His contribution was adequate but not nearly what I had expected. I feared that the Francis embargo on thinking was taking hold.

In the meantime, Chuck Alexander, a friend of mine and admirer of Park, had approached me about doing a five-minute radio show during the playoffs with Brad. We would do about six five-minute segments, discussing the various players and teams that were to meet in the Stanley Cup round. Then, if the Rangers progressed to the semi-finals and finals, we would continue the taping. Park was agreeable and both of us joined the American Federation of Television and Radio Artists.

The NHL had some cockeyed regulation forbidding players to do radio or TV shows during playoff time, and there was talk that Francis would object. But Brad still was sufficiently independent from his boss—I think he still felt the sting of the September contract hassle—and said he was agreeable to the radio deal as long as it didn't conflict with practices and road trips.

New York finished second, behind Boston, in the East Division and was to face fourth-place Toronto in the opening playoff round. At that time my wife Shirley, was battling to obtain membership in the NHL Writers Association and was being rebuffed, intimidated and generally insulted by the male hockey-writing fraternity.

When it was clear that Toronto would meet the Rangers, Shirley got an assignment from the Toronto *Star*. The family page editor of the *Star* wanted a story on hockey wives from the Toronto area and their life-styles at playoff time. Normally this would have been an easy and pleasant story to handle. Brad and his wife Gerry lived in Toronto during the off-season. Walt Tkaczuk's wife lived near Toronto as did Tim Horton's family. Shirley phoned Gerry Park, Valerie Tkaczuk, Nancy Ratelle and Lori Horton and got some beguiling views into their lives without crossing into the realm of catty gossip. After three days of interviewing and researching, Shirley was ready to write the piece. She needed one additional bit of information from Ms. Ratelle and phoned her.

"I'm afraid you can't use any of the material I gave you," Ms. Ratelle informed Shirley. "Mister Francis does not want any of the wives to talk with the press until the playoffs are over."

I was incredulous. I advised Shirley to phone Gerry Park; surely she would lift the embargo. Shirley called and as she talked a stunned look came over her face. Obviously fearing retribution from Francis, Gerry said she was sorry, but Shirley could not use any of the material she had given her. The same was true with Valerie Tkaczuk.

By contrast, Lori Horton said, in effect, that Francis knew what he could do with his bans. She allowed Shirley to use her quotes and the resultant story was a gem, especially since it zeroed in on Francis' idiotic attempt to muffle a perfectly innocent story. Later, Brad allowed that Francis had gone "a bit too far."

What irked me was that none of the players—all of whom I had vigorously supported in my *Sporting News* column at the time of their contract battle—had so much as lifted a finger in support of Shirley. Actually, I was not surprised at Tkaczuk, who had always been rather aloof. But I couldn't believe Ratelle would stand by so quietly, and I was thoroughly disgusted with Park's role—or non-role as it developed. He could have told his wife to ignore Francis the same way Lori Horton did. As Brad later pointed out in *Play the Man,* Ms. Horton not only gave an interview but also posed for pictures at the Garden wearing hot pants. "And," Brad concluded, "Francis didn't do a thing."

Later Shirley asked Francis about the wives' no-talk edict. His lame excuse was that he didn't want them disturbed during the playoffs, from which you could assume that an interview would be fine with him along about June!

That episode, and another incident in which Rangers publicist John Halligan "courageously" evicted Shirley from the Garden press box, made it clear that we had just about reached the end of the line with Rangers management, especially Francis, who obviously was calling the shots. I wondered how this would affect my author-subject relationship with Brad. The answer—that so far it hadn't—came during one of our recording sessions for the Stanley Cup radio show. Brad and Gerry arrived together and were as pleasant as ever. The taping went well, and then the three of us drove out to the Park's Long Island apartment for another book interview.

(This was the first time I had ever driven with Brad, and I was astonished, and frightened, by what to me was his somewhat reckless handling of the car. He seemed totally unconcerned about speed, and by the time we had turned off the Belt Parkway, I was a nervous wreck although I concealed it well.)

It turned out later this was to be our last serious interview together. By now we had covered just about every element in Park's life and his ideas about the world around him.

The Parks and I had dinner, talked some more, and then Brad and Gerry drove me to the station where I caught a train back to New York. The moment I closed the door of their car behind me I felt distinct relief. Our association was becoming a bit trying and, although that interview was productive in a way, I couldn't get rid of the feeling that Francis was somehow impeding Brad's freedom to talk and thereby threatening the success of the book.

But I had gathered plenty of meaty material, especially regarding the in-fighting over the negotiations and the long blast against the Bruins. A strong showing in the playoffs and a Stanley Cup victory would make the ideal ending. Now it was up to the other twenty members of the Rangers to cooperate. The Rangers, after a brief scare, eliminated Toronto in the opening playoff round and then went up against the Chicago Black Hawks, a strong team but one that could be mastered with the proper strategy.

It was an exciting and extremely close series. One game, in New York, was decided in the third sudden death overtime period on a Rangers goal by Peter Stemkowski. Fortunately—I thought—for the book the series went a full seven games. Unfortunately, Chicago won the final game and the Rangers, once again, were out in the cold.

Well, I wasn't completely crushed. After all, this meant that Brad would be free once more to do a final and juicy taping. But suddenly he *did* become difficult. He returned to New York, did a last radio-show taping with me but begged off on any more interviews for the book, claiming it was too soon after the Chicago debacle. Without getting testy, I suggested that we were up against a deadline. He promised that he would take his recorder with him on vacation with the other players and would air mail the cassettes to me.

In the meantime, I began writing. It started off with a

173

bang. Brad had more than done his homework in the opening months and the negotiating hassle was as intimate and revealing as anything ever written about player-management relations in hockey. My concern was that the book would tail off from that point on, but I was reassured as I went over Brad's unabashedly honest material on Francis, the Bruins and other sensitive subjects. I knew the book wouldn't have the near-scandalous quality of Sanderson's *I've Got to Be Me* (Brad had read Derek's book and was suitably appalled by its contents) but it wasn't meant to be pungent in that sense.

At last I reached the final portion—March, April and the two playoff series. All of a sudden, it seemed as if these tapes—which I was hearing for the first time—had been done by a bored schoolboy. People and topics were treated with utter superficiality, impressions were sketchy and everything that had been so good about the other tapes suddenly was missing.

I tried to tell myself it was playoff tension and that Brad would make up for the emptiness with a truly exciting final tape. Day after day went by without hearing from him. Finally, I got word that he was coming through New York enroute to Toronto. We would be able to spend one more evening together and wrap things up.

His plane was almost three hours late, and he and Gerry arrived at the hotel extremely tired and just short of irritable. I wasn't feeling much better myself. So, while our wives chatted on the side, Brad and I discussed the final chapters and came off with practically nothing. His memory had just about gone blank. He was terribly fatigued, and after an hour or so of verbal sparring, Shirley and I said our good-byes.

I arranged to finish the book and then go over the few loose ends via telephone. But now I was in a real bind. Sanderson's book had the perfect ending—the Bruins won the Stanley Cup. Park's book had *no* ending. Even worse, I wondered just what would happen when Francis took a look at the manuscript—and what Park would do after Francis blew his stack as I was sure he'd do.

Just when I had exhausted every possible way of giving the book a punchy climax, I got a much-needed break. Jack Kronis, a retired clothier from Kitchener, Ontario, who frequently sent me hockey clippings of interest, dispatched a story from the Kitchener-Waterloo *Record*. It told about Jim Krulicki, a young hockey player who had skated for the Rangers alongside Brad—before being traded to Detroit. The headline read: "Jim Krulicki Quits Pro Hockey."

Although he was close to Brad's age and had a bright future in the NHL, Krulicki said he was fed up with the structure of professional hockey. "There's no freedom," he said. "Sure the money is good, but money isn't everything . . . . Time is not your own. You can't relax. I don't want to be a machine which can be traded on the whim of people who sit around and discuss what I can do and what I can't do on a hockey rink."

The more I read, the more fascinated I became. Krulicki sounded like a sensitive Derek Sanderson. "Very few people accept an athlete as a person—or even try to," he said. "There's too much phoniness . . . . Professional hockey is a ruthless business and the fun is gone out of the game." Krulicki went on to explain how he had been compelled to play when injured and how he had been ridiculed because of his affection for reading "heavy" stuff. He was, in fact, almost the antithesis of Brad Park.

I saved the article and eventually tracked down Park, read Krulicki's comments to him and asked for his reaction. As I had hoped, Brad semi-sympathetically demolished his former teammate's points one-by-one. It was like a super patriot following a hippie in a debate about Americanism. "At twenty-three," said Brad, "Krulicki and I each made our choice. He selected the 'mod' approach, and I don't blame him. Except I'm more traditional. I accept hockey's minuses as well as its pluses. The game is no honeymoon. It's fun but it's also so incredibly grueling that I've been tempted to become a beachcomber.''

The Krulicki putdown was precisely what I had wanted to bring the book to a close while endorsing the "great game of hockey." Clarence Campbell couldn't have said it better. Brad, once again, was beautiful:

"But then I think of the time and effort I've expended to fulfill my life's ambition—to play in the NHL—and I realize there's merit to the words, 'Sweet are the uses of adversity.'

"For Jim Krulicki, retirement from professional hockey is probably the best thing. But for Brad Park, who expects to be around another ten years or so at the very least, he'd like a spot of champagne from that Stanley Cup!"

That did it. *Play the Man* was complete. Now, for the real excitement—to see whether Francis would try to kill the book.

Frankly, I was more worried than ever. Shirley's and my relationship with the Rangers front office had deteriorated beyond repair. She had taken her case against Madison Square Garden to the New York City Human Rights Commission and won the right to sit alongside men in the Rangers press box.

Francis, Halligan and the jock-sniffing male writers had lost. I had never known Francis to take losing gracefully, and I braced myself for trouble. Fortunately, my editor, Peter Weed, was as determined to print the book, as written, as I was. He was a powerful aide during those early summer days when I needed it most.

Another who became especially helpful was Larry Rauch, an attorney and a former professional baseball player who was one of Brad's closest friends and who seemed to have replaced Pro Sports Inc. as his representative. Larry read the manuscript and was delighted with it. Whenever there was a problem about locating Brad, Rauch would track him down.

I finished the book early in June and sent it to Weed for editing. The manuscript was to be put into print after Park had read it and made any necessary changes—and, of course, after Francis had his say.

Later that month my father suffered a stroke and was hospitalized. The Park book was completely forgotten as I traveled regularly to and from the hospital and my mother's apartment in Brooklyn. From time to time a question about the book arose and I discussed it with Rauch, who knew my dad was ill, and Weed. I think I spoke to Brad only once or twice in that period.

At first my father's condition seemed to improve, but a week after he entered the hospital, he suffered another stroke. Again he appeared on the mend, but by the second week in July the strokes became more frequent and his condition worsened. He found it more and more difficult to speak, to walk and to use his hands. On my last visit to him before he completely lost his speech, I read him a story I had written for *Sport* magazine. Every paragraph or two, he seemed to close his eyes and go to sleep. I would stop but Dad would open his eyes again and say, "Keep going. Keep going!" Those were his last words on this earth.

He died on July 31, 1971.

It was several weeks before I recovered from the loss of the man who had introduced me to hockey and who had rooted so hard for me in those early, tough writing years. After the funeral and mourning period were over, Shirley and I took a three-week motor trip to Quebec and Canada's Maritime Provinces. We returned early in September, and prepared for the last bit of editing before the book went to press.

By now, any closeness that I had once felt with Park was gone. One incident—or non-incident, as it were—clinched my opinion. After my dad's death, I received the usual

177

number of condolence cards and sympathy messages; I even received one from Larry Rauch, whom I hardly knew.

But I never heard from Brad Park.

As far as I was concerned, we had become business acquaintances, no more, no less. I had absolutely no desire to extend our relationship any further. Meanwhile, a book had to be published, and Weed informed me that Park had read and approved the manuscript, making precious few changes.

"What about Francis?" I asked.

"He got a copy of the manuscript," said Weed, "but he hasn't read it. We made sure he received it on September 9th at training camp."

Francis' fast approval became vitally important. The longer we waited for him, the later the book would be printed and the later it would come out. Except that Weed was no fool. According to Park's agreement with his manager, Francis was to *see* the manuscript. There was no agreement to let him change it.

"To hell with him," said Weed. "If Francis wants to make any changes they'll have to be made on the galleys at the last minute."

Francis didn't react until October 15, more than a month after he was sent the copy. According to Weed, Francis wanted the book killed. "Brad is very concerned," Weed told me. "Apparently Francis has bitched quite a bit about it."

My worst fears were realized.

"What are you going to do?" I asked.

Weed assured me that there was no question they would print the book anyway, but he would meet with Park in Francis' office and hash out the problems. It was deemed that my presence at the meeting would be less than prudent, so I remained out of the picture. Shortly after the conference Weed called. He related that Francis complained bitterly about the book and came on very strong. But Peter added (and Brad later confirmed) that he counterattacked twice as hard, and Francis appeared impressed by that. "He said that he objected to 100 things in the book," Weed told me. "He claimed that the facts were wrong, that the sport was being defamed and a few other things."

After the fur had flown back and forth across Francis' office, it turned out that the general manager recommended that only *one line* be deleted from the manuscript. It dealt with Park's description of the Fourth Estate where he says, "All newspapermen are slobs." As Weed recalled, Francis told Park that that would be an imprudent remark, to which Brad shot back, "But it's true!" I asked Weed what he thought of Francis. "The poor fellow," said Weed. "isn't aware of what's being written and done in this world."

The last hurdle was cleared and the book went to press. It made the stores just before Christmas and had difficulty getting off the ground. Park simply wasn't as exciting a personality as Bobby Orr or Derek Sanderson. For the first two months *Play the Man* was a distinct disappointment.

Part of the problem, as mentioned earlier, was the fact that he was a New York player and it was difficult to promote a New York hockey book. But that was only one of the difficulties. It was a damn good book, but I felt the best parts weren't getting enough press exposure. To me the meat was in Park's many blasts at the Boston Bruins. I thought that if the Boston press was made more aware of the contents, they'd write reams of copy about the book.

Dodd Mead agreed, and within a month a full-scale feud had erupted between Park and the Bruins. When Brad played alongside several Bruins in the All-Star Game they made a point of ignoring him. "I hated sharing the dressing room with that creep Park," said Johnny McKenzie. "His presence took all the joy out of being an All-Star." Phil Esposito, Ted Green and even the usually non-controversial Bobby Orr took verbal cracks at Park, and every time they did another story appeared plugging *Play the Man*. By

179

March, Park was the most hated hockey player in Boston and the book began selling like *I've Got to Be Me*.

I was delighted, but Francis and the other Rangers were livid. They claimed that *Play the Man* was to the Bruins what a red flag is to a bull. And the Bruins proved it by demolishing the Rangers in five straight regular season games after the book hit the stands.

"There's no doubt that Park's book helped us more than it helped the Rangers," said Bruins coach Tom Johnson. "It gave our guys extra incentive to beat them. I wonder, though, if Brad realizes how much the things he said in his book can hurt him and the Rangers. He's certainly entitled to his opinions, but he's lost respect among his fellow players for the things he wrote."

Probably not. In any event, Park gained respect in my eyes as the hullabaloo grew louder and louder. He could have copped out. Other athletes have done so, claiming they were misquoted or that the ghostwriter had inserted lines after he had approved the manuscript. Park could have bent to Francis' side and blasted me right off Publisher's Row.

He didn't. "I wanted to write an honest hockey book," Brad told them. "I wanted to tell it like it is, not like it should be or how people want it to be."

Perhaps that, more than anything, was what made working on *Play the Man* all that worthwhile.

XII

THE CON MEN
AND
SHIT MERCHANTS

"Hockey players are the biggest con men and shit merchants I've ever met," my old friend Charlie Barton said to me a couple of years ago.

Barton, who covered hockey for the Buffalo *Courier-Express,* loved the game with a passion matched by few men. He would cover a Buffalo Sabres game on a Sunday night and then on Monday, his night off, show up at a Junior B match in Stamford, Ontario, or Oakville or Waterloo simply because he loved to watch a hockey game. It was Charlie's religion whether he was writing, talking or, I imagine, sleeping.

"Hockey," wrote John MacFarlane, a Canadian editor, "is the Canadian metaphor; the rink a symbol of the country's vast stretches of water and wilderness, its extremes of climate, the player a symbol of our struggle to civilize such a land."

Barton would have put it another way, but the feeling, like MacFarlane's and mine, is mutual. It is a game to be loved—and hated. Hockey and hockey players have changed with society. MacFarlane teamed up with athlete Bruce

Kidd and wrote a book called *The Death of Hockey*. They lamented the cancer of professionalism that afflicted what once was a lovely homebred sport. "We sold it cheap to absentee owners," they wrote, "and saw our Prime Minister humiliated by U. S. owners .... We let a handful of rich and greedy men convert a great sport into another branch of American show business."

Once the game wasn't loathed as it is now by MacFarlane, and the players weren't called "con men and shit merchants," as they were by Barton. When Frank Boucher signed his first NHL contract with the Ottawa Senators in 1921, it never occurred to him to bring along an agent. "I signed a one-year contract for $1,200," said Boucher, "and I considered myself very lucky and happy to be playing hockey. It's not that way anymore. Today, hockey players are all business."

They also are spoiled silly. When Phil Esposito and Bobby Orr of the Boston Bruins were invited to a sports banquet in Manchester, New Hampshire, a few years ago, they refused because the host, Leo Cloutier, wouldn't pay them $1,500 apiece. "I just wanted them to take a bow and say a couple of words," Cloutier lamented, "and they asked for $1,500."

Milt Schmidt, general manager of the Bruins who signed Esposito and Orr, allowed that he simply could not understand such reasoning. "When I was an eighteen-year-old kid," said Schmidt, "I'd go to banquets, say thanks for inviting me, and then sit down."

The change has been brought about primarily because of hockey's surging popularity and egregious dearth of talent. It's a hockey player's market nowadays. They know there aren't enough bodies down in the minors, so screw everybody—coach, manager, fans and writers. One time Charlie Barton told me how upset he was about today's players. I asked what had happened to make him feel that way. He explained that Buffalo's then manager-coach George "Punch" Imlach had just been hospitalized with a possible heart attack. "Some of the guys on this club can't stand Imlach," said Barton. "So, do you know what these animals did? They laughed when they heard that Imlach was in the hospital. Then, one of them noticed Imlach's photo in the paper. He grabbed the paper and burned it."

The coach, who once was absolute ruler of his hockey bench, has been reduced to a servile door-opener. Heaven forbid that a player make an awful mistake. It's almost impossible for a coach to vent his wrath anymore. "I *have* to be calm," said Fred Shero, coach of the Philadelphia Flyers. "If I get mad, I'll wind up saying 'You get that right *or else!'* So they'll look at me and say 'Or else *what?'* And I'll be stuck for an answer.

"The *excuses* you hear sometimes. One guy tells me the reason he's not skating well is because he hasn't got a pair of skates. I couldn't believe my ears. The guy could go out and buy any pair he wants made to measure and have the bill sent to the team. Instead, he borrows a left skate from one player and a right skate from another. I only found out by accident. I swear, you could cry sometimes. You feel like a camp counselor."

Many observers of Team Canada's boorish behavior in the 1972 series with the Russian National Team believed the Canadians played like a collection of raggamuffin kids who had been thrown out of grade school. During an exhibition game in Sweden the NHL stars also were branded as hooligans, and that was giving them all the better of the critique. Such behavior surprises fans raised on pulp magazines, but it was hardly a revelation to insightful Canadians such as Dennis Braithwaite, a Toronto daily *Star* columnist. Braithwaite argued that anyone upset about Team Canada's violent exhibition either was "putting on airs" or didn't know anything about the real nature of

Canadians. By any international standard, Braithwaite explained, his countrymen are "a crude, semi-civilized people." His findings are based on the wild behavior of Canadian troops in World Wars I and II.

"One time," said Braithwaite, "two of our Jeep drivers pulled their revolvers in a Brussels bar and ordered all the patrons out on the street. Just for the hell of it. Any ex-serviceman can tell you stories like these or wilder ones.

"Canadians, as everybody knows, are the world's worst drinkers, holding to the idea that the purpose of libation is to get stinko and then start looking for the action. I have seen rumbles in Timmins beer parlors where the combatants literally came flying through the windows just as the police riot squad arrived."

This, then, should help somewhat to explain why Charlie Barton called hockey players con men and shit merchants, although Braithwaite put it somewhat differently: "Do not from such as these expect finesse; it is in the Canadian psyche to bash heads and wreck furniture. This is how we realize ourselves and make statements for all the world to hear. For good or ill, we're a nation of knuckleheads, of brawn unencumbered with brains.

"Hockey, we always thought, was that kind of game, our kind of game, and no one could ever beat us at it. Alas, those Europeans have taken that game and turned it into something else, a contest of skill and grace no less. That, of course, lets us out."

Unfortunately for pampered hockey players hiding behind their cocoon-like image, there always seems to be some muckraker or gadfly journalist around to disturb their reverie. One such gentleman was Jim Brosnan, the former Cincinnati Reds relief pitcher-turned author. Brosnan, who wrote the highly readable *The Long Season* and *Pennant Race,* once wrote an article for *Maclean's* called "The Hairy

Hawks of Chicago." Many reviewers enjoyed the piece, and so did Lester Pearson, then the Canadian Prime Minister.

Several members of the Black Hawks did *not* like the article, including Stan Mikita, who was described as resting his head on a bar while nursing a hangover. Others condemned Brosnan for the most picayune reasons, including a line which noted that Chicago Stadium had the worst ice in the NHL. Instead of accepting the article as a piece of candid reportage, the Black Hawks screamed bloody murder. A few phoned Brosnan to tell him off and one described the article as a "stab in the back." Black Hawks general manager Tommy Ivan described it as "lies and distortions."

Brosnan, who believed that he had written a well-intentioned and fair piece, was demoralized by the response. But he soon realized that hockey people, unlike the rest of the citizenry, live in an igloo all their own. "Tommy Ivan," said Brosnan, "wanted me to say that hockey was the greatest sport in the world! I wouldn't say that even about baseball! I'm not a public relations hack."

Toronto *Globe and Mail* columnist Scott Young, a friend of both Brosnan and Ivan, intervened. He phoned Ivan to inquire about the roots of the rhubarb. The Black Hawks' manager complained that he had "laid out the red carpet for the guy, and then he does this to us!" Young, one of Canada's most accomplished newspapermen, tried to reason with Ivan in objective, worldly terms, which usually is a mistake when dealing with hockey men. "I tried to persuade him," said Young, "that in the light of what else goes on in hockey, no permanent damage could ensue. More important, were the facts in the article true? As far as I could gather, in a meeting with Ivan later, most were. It was Brosnan publishing them at all that had offended him."

What hurt more than anything was the truth—no more,

no less. Young later asked the opinion of Eric Nesterenko, one of the most intelligent of the Chicago players. "There's a sort of fraternity among pro athletes," said Nesterenko. "We accepted Brosnan on that basis and let him get a lot closer to us than we would anyone else—such as a sportswriter. I thought he sensationalized what he saw and took advantage of us."

I shared Young's view of the article: thoughtful people reading it would find the Black Hawks that much more endearing and human because of it. All Brosnan did was underline the point in a rather eloquent and colorful manner. "I'm afraid," Young concluded, "that the lesson is one applicable not only to hockey. Few people are prepared for realism, or for any art form that projects realism, when they themselves are the subjects."

Canadians—not to mention a majority of American hockey fans—have found it extremely difficult to accept the realism of professional hockey. Canadians had freely predicted that Team Canada would wipe out the Russians eight games to none in their September 1972 confrontation. Instead, the Canadians just barely won the series four games to three with one tie. To the hockey nuts, this was a singular triumph and a victory for Canadian nationalism. Those who could see things clearly and see them whole thought otherwise.

"I refrain from asking what would have happened had Team Canada lost," said Canadian poet Irving Layton, who teaches at York University. "Mass suicides across the country, still proving, though in a more macabre way, that we are a nation one and indivisible? Perhaps, but I'd like the youngsters of this country, beginning with my own eight-year-old, to be given a nobler ideal of heroes to be emulated than the inarticulate specimens I saw stepping up to the mike to receive the frenzied ovations of the crowd."

Moved to still further dissent against the NHL hockey

players, Layton took to verse and wrote a poem based on Team Canada's performance against the Russians. He called it "Portrait of the Artist as a Young Bull."

Looking like an old bull suffering
from hemorrhoids the Minister of
Health
warmly complimented the other
bulls;
artists, he called them, really
artists
And our very best, our very *own*

I thought of them pawing
the ground with their hockey sticks
and of the fine
melancholy face of Solzhenitsyn.

Others were less poetic. Josef Kompalla, the West German referee, described the Canadians as hooligans on ice. Kompalla charged that the Canadians behaved badly off the ice, too. In hotels, he said, they "harassed visitors." Lasse Lilja, coach of the Dutch national team, also was appalled at the poor condition of super star Bobby Orr, who, sidelined because of a knee injury, had gotten out of shape. "Why, he must weigh 200 pounds," Lilja exclaimed. "He has a belly on him like I have, and I haven't played for five years."

Even the Canadian edition of *Time* magazine got into the act, describing big-league hockey players as adolescents on the last frontier. "Most of the off-ice behavior of NHL players is only slightly less boisterous than their mayhem-filled minutes on the playing surface . . . . Organized hockey is a male holdout; the place of women is to adorn training camps, hotel lobbies and a few NHL hotel bedrooms. (In Vancouver, a radio station volunteered to tell coach Harry

187

Sinden the names of four players spotted in an after-hours club.)"

It is in the area of sex, of all things, that hockey players live up to Barton's con men and shit merchants label. Most players would like you to believe that they are a collection of All-Canadian boys, dedicated to their wives or, if they are single, who spend their nights reading Boy Scout manuals.

"When people think of Rod Gilbert," Rod Gilbert once said, "I like them to think of me as a good hockey player who's an inspiration to young kids." Once when a New York *Post* columnist depicted Gilbert as a swinging bachelor who makes better passes at chicks than he does to his teammates, Gilbert reacted as if he had been indicted on sixty-nine counts of sedition. "That column hurt," he complained, "because it attempted to destroy the whole sacrifice I made to create an image of respect. I don't want kids to develop into hippies and I don't want them to think of me as a hippie."

Actually, any serious attempts at image-building have almost single-handedly been destroyed not by writers but by player Derek Sanderson, who has apparently done more to make hockey a sexy sport than anyone else. For instance, at a session with several reporters in Boston early in 1973, Sanderson was asked if he'd mind being traded from Boston to Montreal.

"I'd *love* to play for Montreal," he said with a laugh. "It'd be nice to get laid in Montreal again."

Then someone asked him about the brief period he'd played for the Philadelphia Blazers of the World Hockey Association. In responding, Sanderson complained about Sherbrooke, the Quebec town where the Blazers trained. But his gripe had nothing to do with ice conditions or the local fans. "Awful," he said. "I had to import my own hooker from Montreal while we were there."

That session in Boston took place at Daisy Buchanan's, one of four bars in which Sanderson has a financial interest. The newsmen there included Mark Heisler of the Philadelphia *Bulletin,* Tim Burke of the Montreal *Gazette,* and George Kimball of the avant-garde weekly Boston *Phoenix.* Heisler and Burke, writing for conservative dailies, were reluctant to print most of Sanderson's candid comments. Kimball had no such qualms. The quotes above are from his report, as are these remarks:

"I'd noticed that the Montreal writer had a tendency to wince whenever Derek mentioned something like the bit with the hooker, and it hadn't escaped Sanderson's attention that the fellow had a tendency to omit such items from his notes. After a few hours of some very serious drinking he [Burke] still hadn't loosened up much, which seemed important only because I noticed that Derek, at the bar to pick up the next round, was engaged in conversation with a young lady who is known around Daisy's for reasons entirely devoid of irony as The Fellatio Queen She was looking in our direction.

"Sanderson returned to the table with the drinks. 'Would any of you gentlemen care for a blow job in the back room?' he asked. I thought Tim Burke was going to fall out of his chair."

Members of the Philadelphia Flyers' front office had nearly fallen out of *their* respective chairs two years earlier when the slick, highly respected *Philadelphia* magazine hit the stands in February 1971 with a collection of anecdotes far to the left of licit. Written by Maury Levy, an editor of *Philadelphia,* the article opened with a story about how a well-appointed, middle-aged lady of obvious wealth asked the wife of the Flyers' trainer if she'd agree to a trade. The matronly lady offered her automatic dryer for defenseman Ed Van Impe's *jockstrap.* The deal eventually was consummated when the lady specified that she wanted the inner not the outer jock.

That anecdote unnerved the Flyers officials until they read on to where Levy recounted an episode explaining how sex became a tactic in the Flyers' game plan against the Boston Bruins and, specifically, Derek Sanderson. Levy's subject is Lou Scheinfeld, who then was the Flyers' vice president and has since climbed higher in the organization.

"We had a big game against Boston on a Saturday afternoon," Levy quoted Scheinfeld. "They flew in here the night before with nothing to do. Well, I figure their biggest threat is Sanderson, and everybody knows how much he likes good-looking girls. So I get him this unbelievable broad and tell her to keep him going as long as she can. She even brought along her roommate to occupy another one of the Bruins.

"I called her a little after nine Saturday morning to see what time she got in. 'A few minutes ago,' she said. Beautiful. The game started at 1:30 and Sanderson couldn't have gotten more than two hours sleep, if he got to sleep at all." Sanderson was the star of the game.

Shortly after the article appeared, I phoned Scheinfeld. He denied that he had said those things to Levy about fixing up Sanderson, although he did mention something about a woman who had asked to meet Derek. It was a reasonable denial and left me wondering just how apocryphal the story really was.

When Barton alluded to con men and shit merchants he wasn't speaking of hockey players alone. Charlie had just been burned, as he put it, by Scotty Bowman, coach of the Montreal Canadiens and he wanted to get the matter off his chest.

It seemed the Canadiens and Buffalo Sabres had played a game in Buffalo, which normally would have been covered by the Montreal press contingent that travels with the team. But a severe storm had canceled flights from Montreal, and

Charlie was asked to cover the game for one of the absent Montreal reporters. At the end of the game, Barton visited the Canadiens' dressing room to interview Bowman. "Apparently," said Charlie, "he thought I was covering only for the *Courier-Express* in Buffalo and didn't think his remarks would reach Montreal."

As Barton told it, Bowman said he would pick Rick Martin, a Buffalo forward, over his own player, goalie Ken Dryden, in the voting for NHL rookie-of-the-year. "Well," said Barton, "I wasn't about to tell him that this was going to appear in the Montreal paper, so I just went upstairs and wrote the piece. The next day it got a terrific play. Naturally, Dryden was unhappy, and, of course, so was Bowman. He had thought only Buffalo writers were there when he said it. Scotty denied saying it which, by my count, was his thirty-second quote denial of the year."

Charlie Barton died before he had a chance to witness the biggest con and shit job ever executed in or out of hockey. That would be Sanderson's expedition to the Philadelphia Blazers of the World Hockey Association, where he signed a $2,500,000 contract, played eight games and then was given $1,000,000 to get *off* the team. By any standards, Sanderson had been promised a huge amount of money, had done virtually nothing, and was paid an astronomical pile just to get him out of town because he had done so little for his new club.

Making the scene even more preposterous is the fact that Sanderson had been given an opportunity to do what he always claimed he wanted to do: become a leader. The coach, John McKenzie, had been injured during pre-season practice and Derek was left in charge of the team. "My first reaction," said Sanderson in a retrospective comment on his behavior, "since I'm a player, too, was to take a day off—get drunk, get laid, have a few beers—but we couldn't do that. Then I had to talk Bernie Parent [the goalie] out of retirement twice ... So all this tension is building up, and finally one day at practice Phil Watson, a fly-by-night scout from the Junior Bs, jumped on the ice with his sneakers on. That did it. I just said, 'Here, take the whistle.' So now he's the coach.'' (That Phil Watson, who was working as a scout and coaching assistant for the Blazers when he took over as coach from Sanderson, was the same Phil Watson who had been my nemesis all those years ago when he was coach of the Rangers.)

Shortly after Watson took over, Sanderson injured his back, wound up in a hospital and spent a good deal of time giving interviews well-sprinkled with putdowns of Philadelphia. By the time he was ready to play again, Bernie Brown, president of the Blazers, said he had had it with Sanderson and eventually gave him his $1,000,000 discharge. Sanderson later returned to the Bruins and finished the season with them—including the Stanley Cup playoffs.

More than any other episode, the Sanderson adventure confirmed what many observers had already conceded as fact; that the contemporary hockey player had become more spoiled, more egocentric, more a con man and shit merchant than any of his colleagues in baseball, football, basketball and golf.

"I blame people like me," said Vancouver *Sun* columnist Jim Taylor, "who've helped create the bubble-gum image and shrugged off the unsavory part with the excuse that there's one in every crowd.

"Ken Dryden—the Montreal Canadiens goalie—and I talked about it, and he made the point that sportswriters who blow the whistle wind up being ostracized by the players we cover. Maybe we've thought of that too often. Maybe we've all got some growing up to do."

Charlie Barton had grown up, but he wasn't around long enough to make his point about con men and shit merchants loud and clear.

XIII

ME AND THE
STANLEY CUP
FINALISTS

When the Chicago Black Hawks and Montreal Canadiens played in the 1973 Stanley Cup final round I had more than a passing interest in the tournament since I had rather close relationships—although in some cases short-lived—with several of the players on both clubs.

Occasionally it was a warm friendship, as with Frank Mahovlich of Montreal—and in others it was warm-to-frigid, the story of my acquaintanceship with Stan Mikita of Chicago.

Watching the Hawks-Canadiens Cup matches therefore left me rooting for some individuals against others and, in the end, for myself because I had placed my reputation on the line by stating unequivocally in the Chicago-based *Hockey Digest* that no team with an Esposito in the lineup—be it Phil or Tony—would win the Cup in 1973. And if either Phil's club, the Bruins, or Tony's team, the Black Hawks, did win the championship I would personally fly to Chicago and eat the magazine in front of the editors and writers and any players who wanted to come around and gloat. Since the Bruins had been eliminated, I was compelled to root for the Canadiens (me) against the Black Hawks (Tony).

To better understand my feelings about the particular players involved in the 1973 event, you can consult the lineup below which explains why I preferred Ken Dryden over Stan Mikita and Frank Mahovlich over everybody.

FRANK MAHOVLICH

My first encounter with this impressive, long-strided left wing occurred during the 1960-61 season when I was doing hockey pieces for *Sport* magazine. Frank, like Bobby Hull, had moved into the National Hockey League amid unusual fanfare and, consequently, much had been expected of him. But he played a relatively minor role in the Toronto Maple Leafs' campaigns for three seasons and then suddenly, in 1960-61, he looked like the greatest hockey player in the world.

Racing from one end of the rink to another like a mighty thoroughbred, the man they had nicknamed "Big M" scored so many goals so early in the season that it appeared a good bet he might become the second man in NHL history to reach the 50-goal plateau; the first being Maurice "Rocket" Richard. The editors at *Sport* asked me to do a profile on Mahovlich and I accepted, but with some uncertainty. I had heard that with each goal Frank was becoming more tense and that the Maple Leafs' management had launched a quiet campaign to shield him from everybody but the writers who traveled with the team. At best, I could probably expect a few yeses and nos and then a quick good-bye; that is, if I managed to get the interview in the first place.

I was lucky. Ed Fitkin, one of the most competent administrators ever to be in pro hockey, happened to be handling public relations for the Maple Leafs. Fitkin and I had become friends back in my publicity days with the

Rangers and have remained friends ever since. He contacted Mahovlich and arranged a Sunday morning breakfast interview for me at The Commodore Hotel in Manhattan, then the Leafs' official New York base.

I arrived at Big M's room on schedule, and was greeted by his roommate Red Kelly. Kelly, having been around a long time and being a classy sort, sensed that I would want privacy and shortly left. So there I was with the hottest hockey property since Gordie Howe.

I might as well have been with my kid cousin. Frank was a little wary but basically warm and giving. He still had a touch of the hayseed; not surprising since he was not long out of Timmins, in Northern Ontario. One tip-off was his way of giving me confidential information. "Remember," he'd say with a light tug at my shirt sleeve, "this is off-record."

After the third "this is off-record," I debated with myself whether or not to tell this Bunyanesque hunk of hockey player that the expression is not off-record but off *the* record. I decided to keep my big mouth shut.

The interview flowed smoothly for about 15 minutes until Frank looked at his watch. "I've got to go now," he said, sending a chill through my arms right down to my quivering pen. Would I have to make a story out of a 15-minute session that had not even touched on the really pertinent questions? It looked that way until Mahovlich added, "I have to go to church. Why don't we meet in an hour at the dining room?"

My faith restored, I took the elevator to the lobby and talked with some of the other Toronto players until Frank returned. He ushered me into the restaurant and was perfectly candid and articulate throughout the rest of our interview. I found it hard to believe the stories I had heard about his being tense.

We talked for more than an hour. He did appear a bit uneasy at first when my pen scribbled quickly and every so

195

often would peer over my notebook to see what I had written. But by the time we got past the grapefruit he was thoroughly relaxed and remained that way until it was time for the morning constitutional he usually took with his teammates. "Don't forget," he said while shaking my hand, "I don't want you to use anything that was 'off-record.'"

I assured him that I wouldn't, and walked out of the Commodore on a pair of invisible springs. If Frank Mahovlich was any example, hockey players were among the nicest people in the world. I returned home and began a series of prayers that he would score 50 goals.

At the three-quarter point in the season Frank was scoring at a pace that would put him over the 50-goal mark. Then the *Sport* article appeared. From my professional viewpoint at the time it was a good yarn although today I would have done it differently and a lot better. A copy was sent to Frank and he liked it too, especially since none of his "off-record" comments were used. But by this time a lot of stories were being written on him and his play did begin to deteriorate. Opponents shadowed him wherever he skated on the ice and the media tracked him everywhere else. This took its toll and Mahovlich finished the season with 48 goals, two short of tying the record.

Frank was never the same after that athletically or mentally. Over the next decade, he seemed to become more introverted with each season; and his difficulties with Toronto's extroverted manager-coach Punch Imlach also seemed to worsen by the season.

When I interviewed Mahovlich in 1961 he told me that one of his chief concerns was that the fans would expect him to play as sensationally every season as he did in that very special year. When he tailed off, Toronto fans began booing him. And they'd boo him even when he played a good game.

In November 1964, he played a splendid game at Maple

Leaf Gardens but when he skated off the ice there were those Bronx cheers again. Shortly thereafter, he suffered the first of two nervous breakdowns. Frank missed eleven games and returned to the Leafs in December.

His second breakdown occurred in November 1967. This time he missed four weeks of the schedule and there was no doubt that his troubles with Imlach were at least a major part of his problem, if not the entire problem. There was no communication between the two and in March 1968 Big M was traded to Detroit.

Leaving Imlach was like removing a Mack truck from each of Mahovlich's shoulders. In 1968-69, his first full season with the Red Wings, he scored 49 goals and, rather appropriately, *Sport* asked me to do another profile on him.

I hadn't seen him for several years and was curious about his "new" personality. We met in Detroit vice president Jim Bishop's office and Frank delivered a warm, firm handshake when he walked in. He was looking dapper in a sport jacket and a white turtleneck sweater, and seemed even jauntier and happier than he had during our long-ago conversations at the Commodore. He treated me like an old friend and I was filled with pleasure.

The only difference between Mahovlich as a subject in 1961 and 1969 was his *savoir-faire*. He displayed considerably more poise, more polish and more humor—until I mentioned Imlach. His high spirits disappeared and he was just short of sullen when he said, "The years are gone. What's done is done."

Reluctant though I was, I had to prod him further. I pointed out that Imlach had finally failed in Toronto and been fired, not long after Frank had been traded. I asked him how he felt about it. There was a long pause as he teetered between closing his mouth on the abrasive issue and letting me in on his feelings. All of a sudden, he exploded; not at me

197

but at Imlach, wherever he might have been at that moment. "Why didn't they fire him five years earlier when he started all the crap?"

Gambling, I decided to play devil's advocate. "Don't forget, Frank, Imlach was winning at the time."

He just looked at me for a minute. I surmised that he was thinking about all those Imlach years when Toronto should have been number one, but instead just scrambled into the playoffs; and about all the painful years behind him.

"You say Imlach won," Mahovlich said reflectively. "Well, Hitler won quite a bit, didn't he? So the question is, what is winning?"

Frank was traded from Detroit to Montreal in January 1971 and since then has demonstrated what winning is all about: he's played for two Stanley Cup championship teams. And he doesn't even say "off-record" anymore.

STAN MIKITA

In many ways I felt closer to Stan Mikita than I did to most players I had gotten to know in the early Sixties. Our ancestry was almost the same. He was born in Sokolce in the Czechoslovak province of Slovakia and my grandparents came from Mihalovce, not far from Sokolce. Mikita was a testy little guy in his early NHL days and I fancied myself testy in a similar way.

During the 1961-62 season Mikita emerged as one of the craftiest young centers in the NHL, so it was hardly a surprise when *Sport* magazine sent me to Chicago to do a story on him during the Stanley Cup playoffs of April 1962. Johnny Gottselig, a former Black Hawks ace, was the club publicist at the time. Unlike some of the hostile characters running the Chicago press office these days, Johnny went out of his way to help a visiting writer. He arranged for me to interview Mikita after a practice.

We met in a small office in the bowels of Chicago Stadium. Mikita looked like a member of Hell's Angels. He had just emerged from a post-skate shower and his black hair was gleaming wet and combed back into a duck-tail coiffure. He wore a Black Hawks blazer, except that on him it resembled one of those typically Canadian rink-rat outfits you expect to see in towns like Flin Flan, Manitoba or Crows Nest Pass.

No warming-up period was necessary. We hit it off on the first question and when Stan learned I was of Slovakian descent, we kept on hitting it off. A big help was my relationship with his teammate, goalie Glenn Hall. For two years before I met Mikita, I had been a good friend of Hall's; I had written a long magazine piece on him and frequently lunched with him when the Black Hawks visited Manhattan. I knew that Mikita had seen me with Glenn from time to time and I knew that Stan and Glenn liked each other. That always helps.

What made the Mikita conversation so special was the ease with which he volunteered information. He leaned back in the swivel-chair, put his shoes casually up on the desk, and told me about that night in 1948 when his uncle and aunt, Joe and Anna Mikita, came from Canada to his home in Sokolce to visit his parents, the Gvoths.

"I had no idea," Stan said, "that years earlier my uncle and aunt, who couldn't have children, had asked my parents to let them have their second child. I guess, to make them happy, my parents had said okay. But I don't think they meant it. Anyway, I was the second child and one night during their visit I came downstairs for some milk and jam, and my uncle reminded my mother of the promise. I started to cry because my mother said I couldn't have anything to eat.

"They thought I was crying because I wanted to go to America. They asked me if I wanted to go back with Uncle

Joe and Aunt Anna and I said sure, why not? It was a chance to see America. My folks really didn't want me to go, but they figured it would be a break for me to get out of Czechoslovakia in those rough days just after World War II."

On and on Mikita talked, too fast for my pen, and I listened, fascinated by his extraordinary saga. After all, were it not for a glass of milk and a piece of bread, he might never be playing in the NHL. He pushed his hair back over his ears and continued, telling me how he first learned about hockey on a street in St. Catherines, Ontario, where the Mikitas lived.

"A few kids were playing in the street," Stan went on. "I looked at them and they looked at me. One of them waved me over. He gave me his hockey stick to shoot the puck. I didn't know how but I wanted to be good right away to please him. So I took the stick, swung like I was hitting a golf ball and whacked the guy right in the shins!"

Stan said that that was the first crucial moment in his hockey career. If the fellow was angry, he might have dismissed Mikita as hopeless. "Instead," Stan recalled, "he took me by the hand and showed me with sign language the right way to shoot the puck. Then he taught me my first words of English, 'stick,' 'puck,' 'shoot,' and 'goal.'"

In dealing with athletes, even a pleasant sort like Mahovlich, I had developed a sort of extra-sensory wrist-watch reflex. My mind was always on the clock because players inevitably had appointments of one sort or another, whether for church, a stroll with teammates, an afternoon nap or a pregame dinner, which ended my interviews. With Mikita there was no time limit. He went on and on, talking about everything from the days when his young Canadian friends in St. Catherines put him down with shouts of "D.P." to his current battles with members of other teams.

"Sure I've hit people from behind," Stan admitted

without hesitation. "Who hasn't? There are times when I mean to hurt people. A guy spears me in a game. Then he gives me a cross check, so I give him an elbow. Remember, I'm a small guy, so I figure I got to hit first, before they hit me. When I broke into the NHL I was on a line with Ted Lindsay, a little guy like me. He told me that when I went into the corners, I should keep my stick chest high for protection. And when I throw a pass, not to look where it's goin', but to watch for a guy tryin' to reef me. Once I forgot and Fernie Flaman of Boston damn near killed me. Now, I remember."

It was a smashing interview and a smashing story. Stan talked until I was exhausted and agreed to give me anything else I wanted whenever I wanted it if it would help the article. I thanked him and said I was looking forward to seeing him again.

Mikita was very pleased with the profile when it appeared in *Sport*, under the title "In Hockey, Hit First," and I saw him frequently in the Black Hawks dressing room thereafter. A few seasons later, when I was researching an article on Chicago defenseman Pierre Pilote, I ran into Mikita in a Baltimore hotel the day of an exhibition game. He introduced me to his wife, Jill, a strikingly attractive woman, and we had a pleasant lunch together. Stan surprised me once at the table. I told him I was writing a piece about Pilote and asked him for a couple of quotes. "Pierre is the team captain," he shot back with half a sneer, "and he's management's man." Then, a pause: "But don't use my name with this if you run it."

Our paths crossed again in Manhattan. My friend, Joe Policano, was handling public relations in the United States for the Czech Tourist Bureau, and had arranged two junkets for me to Czechoslovakia. When Policano learned that I was friendly with Mikita he asked if I thought Stan might want to take a trip back to his homeland. I said I didn't know; we had a meeting with Mikita and, for a brief time, it appeared all three of us would be headed for Slovakia. But the deal eventually fizzled out.

My ties with Stan tightened as other friends of mine wrote articles about him with my encouragement. The late Jack Zanger was one. Zanger, who had been an ardent Rangers fan, was so enamored of Mikita and Bobby Hull he switched his allegiance to the Black Hawks. A couple of years later I suggested to *Sport* that a new Mikita profile was in order. Stan had matured; he had won The Lady Byng (good conduct) Trophy and was still a first-rate scorer.

Fred Katz, who had become *Sport*'s managing editor and who was a good friend, liked the idea but asked if I'd mind if he did the piece himself. Katz was intrigued with Mikita and said he had to go out to Chicago anyway. When I said I didn't mind, Katz asked whether he could spend an afternoon with me, picking my brains for questions to ask Mikita when they did their tape-recorded interview. I said that was fine but I also wanted a favor from him. I asked Katz to save the tape so that I could use any of the material after his article appeared. He agreed.

By this time expansion was on us and the hockey-book boom had just begun its early rumblings. I had written a short biography of Gordie Howe and followed that with *Bobby Orr and the Big, Bad Bruins.* One night at a cocktail party I was introduced to Ron Buehl, then an editor for Cowles Book Company. He asked me if I had any ideas for a hockey book. I suggested Mikita. A week later Buehl phoned and said he wanted to do a book on him and he'd like me to write it.

"I'd like to do a first-person (autobiographical) story with him," I suggested. "Mikita and I get along pretty well, and I've known him since 1962."

Buehl agreed that it would be a good idea but he doubted whether his company would approve because Mikita's asking price for an autobiography would surely be out of budget range for what was planned as a teenage book. "You can tell Mikita we'll give him $300 for cooperating with you," said Buehl, "but we really haven't the money for a first-person job."

I spoke to Mikita the next time the Black Hawks were in town and told him about the Cowles project. He said he wanted to talk with his agent and would let me know. We next met at the All-Star Game in Montreal on January 21, 1969, and Stan told me that yes, his agent had an autobiography in mind. I suggested he contact Buehl. The agent and the editor conferred and yes, there was a stalemate.

By now it was late March. I phoned Mikita at home. We had a pleasant chat and then I told him of the deadlock. "I'm afraid," I said, "that if your agent insists on your doing an autobiography I'll have to go ahead with a biography of you on my own. I *am* under contract with Cowles."

Understandably, he wasn't too pleased but there still seemed some vague hope that we might resolve the difficulty to everybody's satisfaction. But later I heard from Buehl that nothing more could be done. He suggested that I get cracking on the book.

Since we had to proceed without Mikita's cooperation, some adjustments had to be made. Instead of running a straight biography, we decided to split the book in half. Half would be Stan's life story and the other would be the first full-length history of the Chicago Black Hawks, a club with a rich and zany background.

For Stan's part, I had to rely on the notes I had accumulated in various interviews with him, and on plenty of research help from friends such as Zanger and Charlie Barton, who delivered a volume of anecdotes going back to Charlie's and Stan's early days in St. Catherines, Ontario. On top of that I had Fred Katz's lengthy tape-recorded interview with Mikita which was the heart of his article. That, as well as interviews with other players, coaches and managers, would provide enough material for the shortened biography.

My book, *Stan Mikita—The Turbulent Career of a Hockey Superstar,* was published in the fall of 1969. Mikita's own autobiography, *I Play to Win,* came out the same season. Both were good books. His was better. I wrote a review commending his job and expected that, while he didn't get any money from the Cowles book, he would appreciate a positive biography about himself the way any other big-time personality would have.

He didn't. Mikita never phoned me, or wrote me to say that he didn't. I found out about it by reading Scott Young's column in the Toronto *Telegram* on May 8, 1971. Mikita blistered me in the column for having the audacity to write a biography about him.

First, Mikita explained about our early meetings and the $300 offer of cooperation. That was all right. What followed was what infuriated me.

"I said thanks but no thanks," Mikita told Young. "I told him (meaning me) about the book George Vass (a Chicago writer) and I were doing and that there didn't seem to be any sense in cooperating to produce a book that would be a competitor to my own."

Mikita had never told me about Vass; nor do I remember him saying anything to me about producing "a book that would be a competitor to my own." Maybe he did, but I don't remember it. But his next line really broke me up. "He [Fischler] said that if I didn't want him to do a book, he wouldn't."

As I later wrote in a letter of rebuttal to Young—who was kind enough to print my side of the story—I informed Mikita that Cowles was going ahead with the project whether Stan intended to cooperate or not. I would never have told Mikita that I would withdraw from the project just because he commanded me to do so. Writing is my business the way hockey-playing is Mikita's business.

I didn't mind Stan's invasion of the writing business but I considered his complaint about a competing book as absurd as *The New York Times* complaining about the *Daily News* competing in the newspaper market. If I was Mikita I would have been *honored* to have a biography on the market; especially since it also contained the first complete history of the Black Hawks between covers.

Mikita also registered a complaint about the jacket copy of my book, particularly one line alluding to the taped interviews. Stan claimed, and correctly I might add, that I never used a tape recorder. But the book was based on taped interviews supplied by Fred Katz. Finally, there was the vague suggestion that Mikita somehow got jabbed because he wasn't consulted on the matter. Obviously, some of the best biographies have been written without the subject's permission, and were the better for it.

Throughout, I had the sensation that Mikita felt I was taking money from hockey players who so richly deserved it. The fact, however, is that I've put lots of money into the pockets of hockey players; especially those with whom I've co-authored books—Rod Gilbert, Derek Sanderson and Brad Park.

So much for my friendship with Stan Mikita. We haven't talked since.

KEN DRYDEN

One afternoon in the spring of 1969 I received a phone call from Paul Marcus, a bubbly fellow with whom I had played ice hockey and who had become an athletes' representative. At the time, Marcus was a junior partner with Pro Sports Inc., headed by Marty Blackman and Steve Arnold with whom I had become friendly.

"I've got somebody you should meet," said Marcus. "He'll be a good story for your *Sporting News* column."

The fellow was Ken Dryden, who had just finished his last game as goaltender for Cornell University and would graduate in June. His brother was NHL goalie Dave Dryden. I was not impressed with the idea even after Marcus reminded me that Dryden was a member of the First All-America Team.

"Paul," I said, trying to be as nice as possible while rejecting the idea, "you know that nobody is interested in a college goalie. We'll probably never hear about this guy again."

Marcus persisted. Dryden was interesting. He was optioned to play for the Montreal Canadiens. He was pleasant. *And* he was a client. I gave in.

We arranged to meet for dinner; three of us, Dryden, my wife and myself. Although Shirley and I hadn't been all that eager to meet with yet another hockey player, it was a warm, lovely evening and we found Dryden most amiable when we picked him up at his hotel.

Derek Sanderson would have suggested The Playboy Club. Brad Park would have settled for The Old Homestead Steak House. Dryden's idea of a good eating place was an unpretentious Middle Eastern restaurant on the Upper West Side of Manhattan called Uncle Tonoose. Over falafel, couscous and tahini, we discovered that this wasn't a hockey player. Dryden was a very aware human being.

That was the year the blacks rioted at Cornell. We talked about the scene there and I timidly asked which side he was on; certain that this big, good-looking Ontario WASP would put down the blacks. Instead, he argued their position, explained several facts we did not find on the pages of *The New York Times* and went from there to some other esoteric topic far removed from skates, sticks and pucks.

Eventually we did talk a little hockey. Ken told me that he was more intent on pursuing his law studies than playing professional hockey. His approach was pragmatic right down the line and I remember thinking to myself that this would probably be the first and last time I'd see this young man professionally. He thinks hockey is a game you play in back yards for fun.

In any event we had the kind of evening you enjoy when you haven't seen a schoolmate for a couple of years. We even tried to get a date for Ken but failed, and we told him to give us a ring next time he was in town.

That was the last I heard from him until the spring of 1971. He had started law school at the University of Manitoba, meanwhile playing for the Canadian National Team, and then he had surprised the hockey world by finally signing with the Montreal Canadiens. Lo and behold, in March 1971 this overgrown quiz kid actually was in the NHL.

More amazing, he started in the nets for Montreal in the Stanley Cup playoffs against Boston. I'll never forget the night I heard about that. Shirley and I and two friends had attended the Rangers-Toronto playoff game at Madison Square Garden and then headed for a little restaurant off Rockefeller Center which had a television set. We knew Dryden was in the nets that night and I feared that the big, bad Bruins would so tar and feather him with pucks that he might never play another hockey game again. He didn't win, of course, but he played capably enough, and although we didn't realize it at the time, a star was born.

He took the Canadiens past the Bruins in a seven-game series, then over the Minnesota North Stars, and finally beat the Chicago Black Hawks in a classic Stanley Cup final that went down to the seventh game before Montreal prevailed.

Meanwhile, I had not seen him since our tête-à-tête at Uncle Tonoose. But soon after the playoffs were over he visited New York to receive "The Life Saver of the Month" award at Leone's Restaurant.

I had no idea whether he would remember me or not, or how he might have changed since his college days at Cornell. I arrived at Leone's while Ken was posing for some promotional photos for Life Savers, and sensed right away that he had added about as much polish to his off-ice personality as he had to his goaltending.

The minute the picture session was over, he turned in my direction and broke into a grin. He *had* remembered, which delighted me no end. We chatted briefly and agreed to get together when the luncheon was over. In the meantime he went about the business of being interviewed by radio, television and newspaper types.

Watching him carefully, I got the feeling that Dryden wasn't out-of-place in this milieu, but he certainly wasn't *in* place. When a reporter would ask the sort of question that would normally elicit a monosyllabic reply, Dryden would expound for several minutes, leaving the newsmen gaping. He talked so much the luncheon was an hour late in starting.

Afterward, Dryden called me over and introduced me to his wife, Linda, a blonde Cornell graduate who seemed as articulate as her husband. We made plans then to spend the coming Sunday doing the town. The Drydens were staying at the Americana Hotel near Times Square. It was a crisp spring day and we picked them up early in the afternoon. "Where would you like to go?" Shirley asked.

"Anywhere," they said and that's where we went. First, down Broadway to the old Woolworth skyscraper, over to City Hall, across the Brooklyn Bridge to Brooklyn Heights overlooking the Lower New York Bay. It was time for a stroll on the promenade facing the Manhattan skyscrapers. Unlike our first conversations, this time the talk turned more readily to hockey. Ken had suddenly become big-time; a household name in Canada and the United States and he knew it. "What do you think I ought to do about getting a representative?" he asked.

I asked about Paul Marcus, whom Dryden had since dropped, but Dryden indicated that he wanted someone more closely related to hockey. Having worked with Derek Sanderson, I knew Bob Woolf quite well. "You won't find an attorney better than him," I said.

By now I had the unpleasant sensation that I was being milked for information by someone who really didn't want to let on that he was milking me. But I didn't mind and, besides, I liked Dryden. "I've been talking to Gerry Patterson," he said. "He handles Jean Beliveau and a few other players. Then there's a guy named McDermott in Boston who's been after me. D'ya know him?" No, I didn't.

To keep our pattern intact we had dinner at another Middle Eastern restaurant, and gabbed on into the night. They seemed like a couple of out-of-town cousins who were spending their first weekend in New York with us—and we were enjoying the tour just as much. After dinner we took them through the Lower East Side and introduced Ken to his first egg cream, the official candy-store drink of New York City. He seemed more impressed by the egg cream than he had been by anything else.

It was clear to me that this brainy boy would be a better subject for a book than Derek Sanderson and Stan Mikita put together. "Have you ever thought about doing one?" I asked.

"Yes," Ken said, "but I don't want it ghosted. I actually want to write it myself."

Good enough. Then, all I'd have to do is edit a bit here and there. He appeared interested enough for me to suggest putting an editor friend in touch with him. "Sure," he said, "I'll talk to him but I don't want to rush things."

In the meantime my wife and Linda Dryden had become good friends. Which says something for Linda because Shirley generally takes a dim view of hockey players' wives. By the time we reached their hotel it was agreed that we'd see each other again soon. A good time was had by all.

On the trip back to our apartment I told Shirley that it was remarkable how little Ken had changed, and how marvelous it was that he seemed so unaffected by the fuss and fanfare swirling around him. I wondered how long it would last.

Within a year I had the answer.

Ken was back in town for another luncheon (at Leone's) and I made a point of getting there. We had spoken several times since his last visit although nothing had developed on the book. As he'd suggested he might, he lined up with Gerry Patterson although he'd phoned me once for more information about the McDermott fellow from Boston who apparently was hot on his trail.

The media encounter was virtually the same this second time around. He talked with the press and then did a few TV and radio interviews. He chatted briefly in between and I asked whether he'd have time to talk after the whole business was over. "Sure," he said, "we'll meet right here."

I'm still waiting for Ken Dryden.

XIV

BROADCASTERS, TELECASTERS AND HOT AIR

Foster Hewitt, then a young reporter for the Toronto *Star,* was the first man to broadcast an ice hockey game. On March 22, 1923, Hewitt's editor, Basil Lake, assigned him to handle the play-by-play of an important amateur match in Toronto between a team from Kitchener, Ontario and Toronto's Parkdale club.

At first, Hewitt, who went on to become the dean of hockey broadcasters, suggested that someone more qualified take the assignment. Since hockey had never been reported on radio before, Lake reasoned that there had never been a hockey broadcaster and, therefore, Hewitt was as qualified as anybody.

"Some thirty or forty years from now," Lake prophesized, "you may be proud to say: 'I was the first person in all the world ever to broadcast a hockey game.'"

Lake was right. Although Hewitt described his first game from inside a foggy, glass-enclosed booth, he survived the experience and created a form of hockey play-by-play that, essentially, has lasted until the present day. Eventually, Hewitt started broadcasting the NHL games from Maple Leaf Gardens and by the mid-Thirties the "Hockey Night in Canada" Saturday night radio shows became the most listened-to program in the entire Dominion and remained so until the advent of television.

Hewitt was the man who captivated me when I first accidentally tuned in my Philco Transitone. I was later told that, as broadcasters go, he lacked several vital qualities associated with first-rate radio men. Mostly, his critics said his voice was bad—too high-pitched.

Well, it *was* high-pitched but that made as much of an impression on hockey fans as a mole on Racquel Welch's leg would to a girl-watcher. Hewitt orchestrated a hockey broadcast the way Leonard Bernstein handled the Philharmonic. His voice entranced listeners and it would reach a crescendo at precisely the right time.

Instead of making the mistake of his contemporaries—trying to say too much—he would compress his report into key expressions seasoned with just the right inflection of anxiety. For example, if there was a frenzied battle for the puck between several players in front of the net, Foster never would waste time trying to identify each one but would, instead, shout: *"IT'S A SCRAM-BLE!"*

His trademark, which has been copied down through the years, was the description of a goal, which often was more exciting in the listening than in the seeing. As I said earlier, it had me ecstatic with tension when I used to listen to those broadcasts.

Hewitt had several other qualities. He knew the game inside out; never had any difficulty identifying players and, as far as I was concerned, was extremely fair. I base this judgement—not shared by all critics—on his handling of the 1950 Stanley Cup semi-final between the Detroit Red Wings and my team, the Toronto Maple Leafs. Leo Reise, Jr. scored for the Red Wings in sudden-death overtime in the seventh game and I can still hear Hewitt's voice booming "HE SHOOTS! HE SCORES!!" as fervently as if Reise was a member of the Maple Leafs.

Unquestionably, the proof of Hewitt's success is his ability to withstand the test of time. He made the successful switch from radio to television although he remained at his best away from the camera. By the 1972-73 season he had slowed somewhat—Foster handled the Team Canada-Russia series on television—but the essential Hewitt still was there and he was the best.

For most of my childhood and young adult life, I yearned for the chance to handle a hockey play-by-play as Foster did. My chance came during the 1954-55 season when I worked for the New York Rangers. The chap who normally broadcast the Rangers games for Armed Forces Radio got sick and I volunteered to handle the mike.

At the time my closest friend on the Rangers was a utility player, Aldo Guidolin (the same who sneaked me onto the train), who very rarely took a regular turn. I hoped Aldo would play on this occasion simply because I wanted to mention his name. "If you do get on the ice," I suggested before game time, "you might consider scoring a goal."

Aldo laughed. "First, let me get on the ice."

New York's opponents that night were the Montreal Canadiens, one of the most powerful teams in hockey. It was a rough game, particularly in the first period and it was all I could do to keep from cursing referee Red Storey during my broadcast. At one point the undermanned Rangers played a man short for four minutes and then received still another penalty.

All of a sudden, who should step on the ice but Guidolin. I figured that he wouldn't be in long so I quickly got in a good plug for him ("Here comes the Rangers peerless penalty-killer, Aldo Guidolin.") and waited for Montreal to score.

The face-off was deep in Rangers territory. The Canadiens won the draw and the puck skimmed out to Boom Boom Geoffrion at the left point. Aldo chased after him but Geoffrion got the puck and wound up for a hard shot. The

213

puck hit Guidolin in his shin pad and rebounded to center ice. Since Aldo was already skating in that direction it was simple for him to break clear.

There I was behind the mike and there was my man, Aldo, on a clean breakaway with half a rink to go before he took his shot at goalie Jacques Plante. I was already leaping out of my seat when Guidolin cruised in from the right and then swerved—it seemed an interminable time—across the goal mouth to the left. Then, at a point when it appeared that he had lost his chance, Aldo flipped the puck into the left corner of the net.

I was so consumed with joy and excitement that I completely forgot that I had shouted *"HE SHOOTS! HE SCORES!!"* and repeated it twice as loud a second time. The Canadiens won the game 7-1 but I had preserved my broadcast on a record, and sent a copy of it to Guidolin as a wedding present.

That experience gave me new ideas about what I had believed was a relatively easy job—hockey broadcasting. It isn't. Too much takes place on the ice for the announcer to spell out all the action, yet that is what all newcomers behind the mike try to do. Then, there is the problem of objectivity; I fear it eluded me in that game although I admit I half-heartedly shouted when the Canadiens scored.

After that, I began to listen to hockey play-by-play men with a more critical ear; and still do. Obviously, they play an important part in the business, yet only a precious few are capable of doing the job well.

Hewitt reigned supreme until the mid-Forties when a tall, husky chap moved behind the mike for the Montreal Canadiens. Unlike Hewitt, Doug Smith had a lower-pitched voice and a unique goal-announcing style that set him apart from the master, but was appealing enough to put him right up at the top with Foster.

If justice were done Smith would still be handling the Canadiens' games—he's now doing pro football in Montreal—but he was eventually replaced because, I am told, of some foolish conflict with a network bureaucrat. Whatever the case, hockey broadcasting lost a winner when Doug Smith left but his replacement, Danny Gallivan, proved to be a more than adequate successor.

Like Smith, Gallivan had a perfect announcer's pitch and a way of saying *"HE SCORES!!"* in a manner that fell just short of Hewitt's. As Foster aged and Gallivan matured, Danny emerged—as he is today—as the best hockey play-by-play man in North America. Hewitt's son Bill, who was broken in at an early age, also moved into a prominent position and virtually became a duplicate of his father; which is another way of saying he is excellent.

Unfortunately, the growth of hockey broadcasting in the United States has lagged far behind the progress made by Canadiens such as Hewitt and Gallivan. Several stations in major league cities have imported Canadians such as Dan Kelly (St. Louis), Tim Ryan (formerly New York), Hal Kelly (Minnesota) to handle the broadcasts rather than let inexperienced Americans get behind the mike.

Dan Kelly handled the CBS "Game Of The Week" telecast for several years and was exquisitely objective and perfectly exciting and accurate. When NBC took over the NHL telecasts during the 1972-73 season, Tim Ryan replaced Kelly. More of a reporter than a screamer, Ryan did a cool, calm and collected job of broadcasting.

The problem with hockey broadcasting in the United States is that quality too often stops with the network play-by-play men. Broadcasters are disgustingly partial. (When Win Elliot handled the Rangers' games he'd frequently report *"WE'RE* ahead, 3-1.")

The root of the problem is that team owners often own the local broadcast too. In New York, for instance, Madison Square Garden—which owns the Rangers—also owns the Ranger television and radio broadcasts from opening face-off to closing buzzer. "That," a WNBC-Radio official told me, "is why the Rangers have been able to bar you from appearing on the between-periods interview show that comes from the Garden."

There are, of course, exceptions to the "house men" routine in the hockey broadcasting business. Marv Albert, who has been the voice of the Rangers for many years, has developed into one of the top three hockey (and basketball) play-by-play men in the United States without rooting; or without rooting very hard. "I believe," Albert told me, "that the sportscaster can display enthusiasm for the home team unless he is on a major network, but even then the side comments and analysis should be without favoritism. The announcer *has* to report when the home team is not doing well and must single out which player gave the puck away or missed the shot."

Interestingly, Marv's younger brother Al handled play-by-play for the New York Islanders, the team from Long Island, during the 1972-73 season. The Islanders were, by most estimates, the worst team in NHL history yet Albert charged the games with excitement and enthusiasm even while reporting the Islanders' ineptitude. That was first-rate hockey broadcasting.

Originally I was to be Al's "color" man (an "expert" who supplies pithy observations during lulls in the action) on the Islanders' broadcasts, at his request. I met with Jack Sullivan, manager of radio station WHN which broadcast the games and explained why he couldn't hire me. "I am the gadfly of the NHL," I told him. "There's no way the Islanders' management would approve me for the job."

Sullivan naively assured me that the station did, in fact, have some say in the hiring and that he would recommend me for the job. Three weeks later, a week before the season opened, Sullivan phoned. "Somebody on the Islanders doesn't like you a lot," he said. "I can't hire you."

I laughed. "Jack," I said, "that's what I told you in the first place. The general manager of the hockey team (Bill

Torrey) decides who's going to do it, not the general manager of the station."

Sullivan erupted. "Nobody tells me who is going to do the broadcasts."

I apologized. "What I mean to say, Jack, is that the Islanders tell you who is *not* going to do the color; and I am not."

They wound up hiring Jack Decelles, an excellent choice. He is a former hockey player and professional broadcaster with a keen insight into the game and a reserve that set him apart from his Manhattan counterpart, Bill Chadwick, who has been the radio and, lately, television color man for the Rangers.

Chadwick is a walking contradiction. A member of Hockey's Hall Of Fame, he was one of the few American-born referees in the NHL and survived 16 years at the job. More amazing is the little-known fact that Chadwick is completely blind in one eye; the result of an injury suffered in his pre-refereeing days when he played amateur hockey.

Hired by the Rangers to assist Marv Albert with the radio color during Ranger games, Chadwick was unusually nervous in his first year behind the mike. He sounded as if he was talking while rolling jellybeans around in his mouth.

His delivery hasn't changed much since then, but Chadwick has lost some of his nervousness and has developed a relatively unusual approach. Instead of delivering the usual "everybody's great" pap so frequently dispensed by most color men, Chadwick frequently singles out players—usually on the opposition—for criticism. More than that, he has no compunction about saying that a game was lousy if he believed it was lousy.

Unfortunately, Chadwick's candor seems to have its limits. Although the Rangers have never won a Stanley Cup during the eight-year stewardship of general manager Emile Francis (who is in a position to fire Chadwick), I have never heard Chadwick criticize him.

217

Chadwick's other weakness is his penchant for playing favorites among the team members. Certain Rangers in particular will be shielded from criticism—and, of course, doused with praise—while others, such as young forward Gene Carr, will frequently be singled out for raps.

My personal grievance with Chadwick occurred when he was still handling only radio coverage with Albert. The Rangers had quietly made it clear that I was not to appear on the between-periods interviews, although I had been making those appearances for more than a decade.

One day I phoned Chadwick at the station to find out whether or not a boycott actually was in effect against me. "Nobody tells me what to do," Chadwick insisted. "If I want you to be on, you can be on. It's just that I'm booked pretty heavy now."

I got the impression that I would soon be back on the air with him, but time went by and Chadwick didn't call. I decided to check the situation out a bit higher on the ladder. From that I got quite a different impression: "The Rangers don't want you so don't waste your time. As long as you write negative stuff about the Rangers you won't be invited on."

With that, I decided to have a showdown with Emile Francis. I made an appointment to see him. At the meeting we talked freely about a lot of things, but mostly I told him that I was sick and tired of all the Gestapo-like harrassment I was experiencing on the hockey beat.

"I've been informed," I told him, "that I have been blacklisted from appearing between periods on the radio shows during the games. Is that true?"

He took a drag on his Lucky Strike, stared up at the ceiling, and put it as plainly as possible: "It's not that you've been blacklisted, or banned from appearing. It's just that we haven't invited you!"

XV

MY MOST
OVERRATED
PLAYERS

Ah, but a man's reach should exceed his grasp.
Or what's a heaven for?

Greatness is in the eye of the press agent and in the typewriter of the home town hack. It is a fact of hockey life that many players are broken before they cut their major league puck teeth by the exaggerated claims of biased newsmen.

What better case than Gene Carr of the New York Rangers. When the speedy, blond forward was traded from St. Louis to Broadway in 1971-72, the man who writes (sic) about Gotham hockey for *The Hockey News* nearly fell over his exclamation points searching for adjectives to describe Carr.

The writer finally settled for "Next Rangers Superstar," and, thus, another overrated player was created. As super-flubs go, the left wing Carr was a gem. He not only produced little but managed to so disrupt the talents of his center, Walt Tkaczuk, that it was a tribute to Tkaczuk's metabolism that he didn't simply whack Carr on top of the head with his hockey stick and leave it at that.

Just to prove he was not an overnight flop but a full-fledged failure, Carr played just as badly for the Rangers through the 1972-73 season and fell down the Chicago Stadium stairs minutes after New York was eliminated from the playoffs. Which should have qualified him for my ten most overrated list.

But it didn't. This special list is reserved for players who have accumulated mountains of press clippings. Carr merely has a hill. It is reserved for those who win places on All-Star teams because hockey writers, as a rule, are ignorant of the sport and therefore vote—giving the home town player a ten-point edge simply because he *is* the home town player—on the basis of league statistics and what they are fed by lobbying press agents, not to mention the players themselves. It is reserved for the very *good* players who mistakenly think they are—and are thought to be by others—great players, never realizing that the last truly great players to skate were Bobby Hull and Gordie Howe.

To make the overrated list a player must have a) failed to live up to his notices and b) not played superior enough hockey. He may be very good, but not great. Such players are therefore overblown, a fact known only too well by the people who pay their salaries. And, sometimes, not even by them. Ready or not, here they come:

Red Berenson, Detroit Red Wings—When he played for the Montreal Canadiens and New York Rangers, he was a big zip. At St. Louis, he emerged as "The Red Baron," the captivating center who once scored six goals against a terrible Philadelphia Flyers hockey team in one game. Shazam!

Thanks to a full color front cover on *Sports Illustrated*, Berenson became "the first expansion superstar." But maybe Emile Francis knew something when he got rid of Berenson. "Red," said Francis, "does not like to get hit. He's shy."

Whatever Red was, the St. Louis brass eventually found

him wanting. They traded him to Detroit for Garry Unger and the Red Wings reacted as if the Messiah had come. "We think," said Detroit manager Ned Harkness, "that Berenson has the leadership qualities we want."

It's no secret. Harkness had hoped Berenson would pick up where the retired Gordie Howe had left off. Detroit needed an on-ice boss. Howe had been one. Captain Alex Delvecchio, thinking of retirement, wasn't. There were fast, gifted kids to be helped. The Redhead would be the new leader.

The Redhead was a bust and in 1973 Detroit failed to make the playoff as they had in 1972. Since the glory days of St. Louis, Red has played the way he did earlier at the Forum in Montreal and in New York's Madison Square Garden. His most outstanding qualities are the color of his hair, the length of his stick and the helmet on his head. I'm not even so sure he was very good at being president of the NHL Players' Association. Fortunately, he was replaced by Ken Dryden.

Tony Esposito, Chicago Black Hawks — Since the Windy City sextet does not have a particularly good press department, one can't charge off Tony Esposito's inflated clippings to the Chicago Stadium flacks. Actually, Tony's best press agent is the NHL Guide, which correctly notes that he won the Vezina Trophy in 1970 and shared the Vezina with teammate Gary Smith in 1972. His average during the 1971-72 season was an awesome 1.76—awesome, that is, if you are easily impressed by arithmetic.

Unfortunately for Tony, the Canadiens never have been too interested in mathematics. The Montrealers have made it abundantly clear that when the hockey chips are down in the Stanley Cup finals, Tony Esposito can be counted upon to lose.

In the 1970 playoffs, even the Bruins discovered Esposito's weak underbelly and blasted Chicago out of the Cup round in four straight games. Tony's average suddenly ballooned. During the 1971 Cup finale against Montreal, Tony fanned on Jacques Lemaire's blue line shot, opening the flood gates for the Canadiens' tidal wave. It was a goal that most goalies would have stopped with ease. Then, in the spring of 1972 Tony went up against the Rangers in the second Cup round and looked like a weak Junior B scrub. And he was not much better in May 1973 when the Canadiens took him six games for the Cup. As far as Tony Esposito is concerned, they've found him out. Good he is, sometimes; occasionally very good; but great he'll never be.

Vic Hadfield, New York Rangers — When Vic Hadfield scored his fiftieth goal of the NHL season in the spring of 1972 against the Montreal Canadiens, the Madison Square Garden regulars reacted as if they had just witnessed the second coming. Maurice "Rocket" Richard could be forgiven if he had vomited at that moment.

If nothing else, Hadfield's fifty goals symbolize the utter cheapness of a goal in NHL hockey today. As the quality has deteriorated with expansion, goals come much easier. It is, in fact, an insult to Richard, not to mention Gordie Howe who never even scored fifty, to suggest that Hadfield is in Richard's class.

Hadfield is a plugging, often clumsy left wing—no more, no less—whose success is made by his center Jean Ratelle and by his right wing Rod Gilbert.

It has been said that Hadfield provides the Rangers with muscle up front. The truth is that Hadfield's match when it comes to fighting has been tiny Henri Richard of the Canadiens. The only trouble being that Richard cleaned Vic's clock a long time ago and Hadfield hasn't done much worthwhile winning in the pugilistic department ever since. Exhibit A was the Derek Sanderson routing of Hadfield in the 1973 Stanley Cup playoffs.

As for his leadership qualities, Vic demonstrated his devotion to the organization when he walked out on Team

Canada in Russia in September 1972. He was then supposed to lead the Rangers to first place and the Stanley Cup. They finished third and were eliminated in five games by Chicago. That says it for Hadfield's leadership.

Garry Unger, St. Louis Blues — He's as pretty as they come and fast and clever with the stick. "As a matter of fact," Gordie Howe once said, "there's nothing that boy can't do."

Not quite. The one thing Garry Unger can't do is put it all together for a long enough time for everyone to say that Garry Unger has finally put it all together. Up to now, they've been saying that he'll be leading the St. Louis Blues soon, if only. . . .

But, then again, they said that years ago when he came to the Toronto Maple Leafs and Punch Imlach thought he had a diamond in the rough. Imlach was right, but Punch couldn't wait, and he traded Garry to Detroit, where Unger's long hair got in the way of manager Ned Harkness' etiquette books, although at one point Harkness implied he valued Unger greatly when he labeled him "an·untouchable."

Garry was touched when he learned he had been dealt to St. Louis. Following Red Berenson's act was not easy, but the blond bomber has outscored Berenson in all the seasons following the trade and had a nice pile of points in the playoffs.

Which is good, but not good enough in relation to the build-up. Garry no longer can use age as a cop-out. He's skated in the NHL since 1967 and he's skating in a league that is more diluted than ever. If he doesn't average far more than a point a game, he's overrated.

Bernie Parent, Philadelphia Flyers — You can still hear the trumpets blasting in Miami — *BERNIE PARENT HAS ARRIVED TO SIGN WITH THE SCREAMING EAGLES.* This was a big breakthrough for the World

223

Slapshot!

Hockey Association. Bernie Parent was skipping Toronto for the new league in January 1972.

Well, the Screaming Eagles never did get off the ground, but Bernie did—in a way. He eventually wound up in Philadelphia with son of Screaming Eagles, the Blazers. The trumpet blast was a little less audible the second time around, but Bernie, to be sure, was to be the best young goalie the WHA had signed—until Garry Cheevers came along.

But just how good is Parent—compared to what he is supposed to be? Back in 1969, they said he'd be the new Mr. Vezina. "Bernie is the best young goalie in the NHL," said Scotty Bowman, who was coach of the St. Louis Blues. "And when Glenn Hall and Jacques Plante retire he'll be the best in the game."

Hall and Plante have retired. But Parent, the best in the game? Not by a Derek Sanderson shot. Parent is a good goalie, but he is weak with his stick—as opposed to New York's Ed Giacomin—and was less than spectacular in the playoffs during his last two NHL seasons.

It was hoped that Parent would infuse the Blazers with color and class. The best he could do in the first month of action was break a foot and wind up in the hospital. But his worst play of all was quitting the Blazers in the midst of the 1973 playoffs.

Keith Magnuson, Chicago Black Hawks — Horatio Alger would have liked this guy. Ketchup-red hair, a disposition to go with it, college diploma, and all that and all that.

Magnuson came into the league with his fists swinging. Then, the other guys started swinging back. "He [Magnuson] couldn't fight his way out of a paper bag . . . he can't lick his lips," said Rick Foley, who teamed up with Keith on the Black Hawks defense for a season.

They accented Magnuson's "fighting ability" because Keith once made the mistake of telling newsmen he had taken boxing lessons from Johnny Coulon. Then, there was that other bit about judo. So, this must be one helluva guy. Right?

Wrong.

Ask Dave Schultz of the Philadelphia Flyers. Better still, remember that game in Philly on November 9, 1972? That was when Magnuson went after Schultz.

"I saw him coming from the side," said the Philly rookie. "I could tell he wanted to start something."

Magnuson did. And Schultz ended it. "He never touched me once," said Schultz.

They met again later. Schultz' arms came up and Magnuson went down, his mouth bloody.

Sure, Magnuson tries hard and he's colorful. But he's a lousy defenseman, and he loses as many fights as he wins. It was no accident that the Hawks played their best defensive hockey in the 1973 playoffs after Magnuson was injured and replaced by Doug Jarrett. And to think that Keith had the nerve to write a book.

Orland Kurtenbach, Vancouver Canucks — You know how certain players somehow develop auras around their personalities. But when you stop to wonder just what the aura is all about you discover that it's just so much cotton candy mixed with printer's ink.

That's the story of Orland Kurtenbach.

In Vancouver, he became some sort of god—"the heart and soul" of the Canucks and, besides, the best damn fighter in the NHL. Bullshoot. Wayne Cashman destroyed the best-fighter myth a long time ago, if Ted Harris hadn't done it earlier.

Anyhow, with Kurtenbach as the heart and soul of the Canucks, Vancouver's somewhat too generous fans have been witnessing a rather moribund hockey team. There was not even hope of a playoff berth in the past three years, and only the dream of one in the future.

As for "Big Kurt," well, he's big and he is Kurt. But he's

also slow and seems always out of breath, apparently made for Western League hockey whence he came.

Paul Henderson, Toronto Maple Leafs — His Team Canada heroics against the Russian National Team in September 1972 concealed—for a time anyway—the fact that this speedy skater really does not fancy the NHL jungle with its muck-muck-muck in the corners.

It's a pity, too, because Paul has several textbook moves and a dynamic overdrive. But his brakes are too powerful when an enemy defenseman looms on the horizon.

When all the Team Canada hullabaloo simmered down and the real Paul Henderson came to the fore, his Toronto Maple Leafs were out of the playoffs again in 1973 and his scoring was so weak that even in this diluted game of the Seventies Henderson averaged less than a point a game.

Bill Goldsworthy, Minnesota North Stars — Now here's living proof of what a good gimmick will do. Bill Goldsworthy, like Orland Kurtenbach, a forward who can barely average a point a game in today's inflationary shinny, managed to come up with a clever little chorus line kick after scoring a goal. One day somebody named it "The Goldy Shuffle."

All of a sudden, Goldy becomes the hit of Minnesota and the high man on the North Stars totem pole. Except he is never that high in the scoring list, where it counts. His thirty-one goals and thirty-one assists in seventy-eight games in the 1971-72 season were all right, but where was Goldy in the seven-game playoff round against St. Louis? A measly two goals in seven games hardly qualifies the man for stardom, wot! And he wasn't much help as Minnesota was wiped out by Philadelphia in April 1973.

And how about Goldy's sorrowful performance in the Team Canada-Russia series when he walked off the ice in Vancouver and said something about being ashamed of being a Canadian? (Naturally, he amended the statement later on, but the bad taste didn't go away all that fast.)

What is Goldsworthy? More than a pedestrian right wing but still far from the celestial plateau of, say, Rod Gilbert. Rod's problem is that he hasn't discovered a shuffle of his own. You can't make it on Broadway with the Gilbert Gimp.

EPILOGUE

A large cardboard box sits on a shelf overlooking my desk. It contains a rich collection of mail dating back to 1958 when I criticized Phil Watson in print for pigheadedness above and beyond the call of duty, even for a hockey coach.

What makes the letters so interesting and significant is the diversity of accusations they contain. There are about a hundred messages accusing me of being an arrogant Rangers fan bent on criticizing Bobby Orr and the Big, Bad Bruins. And there are an equal number suggesting that I have been a not-so-secret agent of the Boston hockey club whose sole mission is to crucify Emile Francis, Vic Hadfield and other members of the most consistent non-championship team in hockey history, the Rangers.

I have been twitted for promoting Brad Park over Bobby Orr and counter-twitted for touting Orr over the entire New York club. I have been accused of being a publicity-seeker and have been charged with trying to become "the Howard Cosell of hockey." (I'd like to get my hands on the varmint who said that!!) Some letter-writers—about one-quarter—say they like my stuff. Most can't understand me. They think I hate hockey (which couldn't be farther from the truth) and have a nagging suspicion that I am passionately against *their* favorite team (which may be true at any given writing but can turn about the next day).

Consistency, as ardent hockey fans define it, is not my bag: A critic's sense of fair play is. I see no reason why I should lavish complimentary adjectives on men like Brad Park, Bobby Orr or Derek Sanderson just because I have written books about or with them. Nor do I see any point in demeaning the accomplishments of a man such as New York Islanders manager Bill Torrey even though he rejected me for a job as announcer for his team's games.

A reader might wonder how I can call goalie Tony Esposito one of my "most overrated" hockey players in one chapter while praising him in another. Simple. He has been a competent player, and I have so stated. But he also has received, in my estimation, accolades far exceeding his accomplishments. For this he deserves a comeuppance, and I have no hesitation in delivering it.

In fact I rather enjoy putting down hockey players these days; much more than I did five or ten years ago. I enjoy it because I don't like hockey players as people as much as I used to. Before expansion, hockey players were among the nicest people in the world. They were important but not self-important. They didn't have agents or attorneys. They weren't overpaid and they considered it a privilege to speak before a kids' group for nothing, whereas today it can cost up to $5,000 to get a hockey player to address a group for an hour.

In the old days a man would consider himself privileged to play big-league hockey. Now, I get the feeling that hockey players think they are doing *us* a favor by letting us watch them. Hockey players have become the spoiled brats of sport and perhaps the greediest athletes since the invention of money.

Bobby Orr, for example, receives $2,500 for a speaking engagement and, according to his personal agent Bob Haggert, he could earn even more. "I'm thinking of putting a $5,000 tag on him," Haggert told the Toronto *Star,* "just to discourage requests for him."

This is the same Orr who, like other superstars, will duck the questions of sportswriters by hiding in the trainers' room and who, according to Haggert, "hates to say no to people."

With some exceptions, the contemporary hockey players remind me a lot of those cops who are always complaining. The cops beef about paperwork, night shifts, street demonstrators, judges and parole boards. Hockey players beef about road trips, long schedules, pesty fans, bad ice, good ice and medium ice. Listening to them, you forget that they *wanted* to be hockey players. They sound as if they'd been drafted for the job.

But don't let me mislead you. I still love hockey and many of the people connected with the game. I love it so much I write about it almost 365 days a year. I love it so much I hate to see it corrupted by the stupidity that sometimes seems as much a part of the sport as the ice.

Yes, I love the game so much that I not only criticize it devotedly, but I also harbor and espouse a long list of impossible dreams for hockey. I believe the slapshot should be abolished so that goalies could give up their grotesque face masks and look like human beings again. If I were the supreme dictator of hockey, I would also abolish helmets. Because if hockey players were as tough as they claim to be, they'd do without those absurd pieces of headgear that make Stan Mikita look exactly like Cliff Koroll and Cliff Koroll exactly like Pit Martin.

Jimmy Cannon said that hockey would be a better game if it were played in mud. That's not true; but it would be a better game if the NHL and WHA bosses allowed the game to be played the way the Russians play it. Then the true skills such as passing, stickhandling and wrist-shooting would emerge once more.

It would be a better game if a $50,000 salary limit were placed on every big-league contract and if the NHL and WHA ended their silly war and merged into one two-league set-up similar to the National and American Leagues in baseball.

I am sure that the objects of my criticism could in turn produce a long list of "shoulds" which would apply to my thinking and writing. But, despite what my critics may think, I have never considered myself an absolute authority on any aspect of The Game. However, I do believe that my background as a political, show biz and general reporter and also as a part-time player has qualified me for opinionating as much as the next man.

And, finally, let it be known that I like what I am doing although it frequently has made my existence downright painful and generally miserable.

But it beats working in stockrooms, the Pentagon, factories, taxicabs, classrooms, mines or courtrooms, to name a few other occupations.

For every pain in the neck like Derek Sanderson, there has always been a good guy like Larry Zeidel or Aldo Guidolin. And whenever some kid comes up to me and asks me how I like my work, I'm inclined to tell him what my friend, the late Charlie Barton, used to say: "I haven't worked a day in my life—I'm a hockey writer!"